Praise for *Culturally Incorrect*

Rod Parsley's new book, *Culturally Incorrect*, exposes the real battle for the soul of America. His straightforward and courageous style will challenge your understanding of the Christian's role in society and help you know what you can do to make a real difference in our world today.

Dr. Jerry Falwell
President and Chancellor, Liberty University, Lynchburg, Virginia

Rod Parsley is a pastor whose love of God and country has compelled him to put pen to paper and issue a clarion call in *Culturally Incorrect*. Throughout this work of the heart, Pastor Parsley exhorts men and women of faith to engage in the culture war over the values we will teach to our children and grandchildren. *Culturally Incorrect* is a must read for anyone who cherishes America's Judeo-Christian values.

Gary L. Bauer
President American Values

One of the important books of this new century. Rise up, O men of God, and put your armor on.

Zell Miller
Former U.S. Senator, Georgia

Pastor Rod Parsley's latest book, *Culturally Incorrect*, is a wake-up call to the Christians of America. The culture war for the soul of America and the future of our children and grandchildren rages on all fronts. Far too many Christians sit in the fog of political correctness and are not engaged in this crucial fight. If you read one book this year, read *Culturally Incorrect*. Join the fight for the future of America.

Pastor John Hagee
Cornerstone Church, San Antonio, Texas

Engaging the heart is Rod Parsley's passion. Who better can be trusted to lead charismatic Christians to engage their part in today's cultural war? *Culturally Incorrect: The Real War of the Worlds* made my spirit leap with joy as a 21st century tone that will help true believers identify God's purpose amidst a lot of political noise.

Star Parker
CURE President

If we are to save America we must win the culture war. Pastor Parsley's new book is an indispensable weapon that will arm Christians as never before.

Paul M. Weyrich
Chairman and CEO, Free Congress Foundation

In this book, Rod Parsley has put together in a clearly understandable way what is happening to the moral values in our society. These changes will affect our families, our children, our churches and our freedom. This book is required reading for every person who is concerned about the future of our country.

Donald E. Wildmon,
Chairman, American Family Association

Pastor Parsley has once again used his literary gifts to challenge our minds and enlighten readers of issues that have attempted to shatter the moral foundation of our country. Brace yourself for a journey of truth!

Bishop Paul S. Morton, Sr.
Greater St. Stephen Ministries, New Orleans/Atlanta
Presiding Bishop, Full Gospel Baptist Church Fellowship International

In Roman times, the Apostle Paul impacted the empire using a reed pen and parchment. His epistles, written from prison, became the Sword of the Spirit to reveal to the infant church an understanding of spiritual warfare and how to win it. After reviewing Pastor Parsley's book, *Culturally Incorrect, the Real War of the Worlds*, I would call it, "The Manifesto for the end time church." Masterfully written and fully documented, his riveting words will thrust you from the back pew comfort zone of western seeker-sensitive Christianity, to the front line of America's cultural clash, armed with revelation knowledge to stand for the truth in these challenging days. This book is a must read and this revelation must be heard throughout North America.

Perry Stone, Jr.
Host of Manna-fest, President of Voice of Evangelism

CULTURALLY INCORRECT

Rod Parsley has written more than fifty books
including his bestseller *Silent No More*. In addition, he
has prepared a *Culturally Incorrect* companion study guide
to assist you or your small group to walk through this
book together. Visit www.rodparsley.com to learn
more about these and other products.

CULTURALLY INCORRECT

How Clashing Worldviews
Affect Your Future

ROD PARSLEY

THOMAS NELSON
Since 1798

NASHVILLE DALLAS MEXICO CITY RIO DE JANEIRO BEIJING

Published in Nashville, TN, by Thomas Nelson. Thomas Nelson is a trademark of Thomas Nelson, Inc.

Thomas Nelson, Inc., titles may be purchased in bulk for educational, business, fundraising, or sales promotional use. For information, please email SpecialMarkets@ThomasNelson.com.

Unless otherwise indicated, all Scripture quotations are taken from *The Holy Bible, New King James Version.* Copyright © 1982 by Thomas Nelson, Inc. Used by permission.

Scripture quotations marked KJV are from the *King James Version* of the Bible.

Scripture quotations marked NASB are from the *New American Standard Bible.* Copyright © 1960, 1962, 1963, 1968, 1971, 1972, 1973, 1975, 1977, 1995 by The Lockman Foundation.

Scripture quotations marked NIV are from the *Holy Bible, New International Version®.* Copyright © 1973, 1978, 1984 by International Bible Society. Used by permission of Zondervan Publishing House. All rights reserved.

Library of Congress Cataloging-in-Publication Data on file.

ISBN 10: 1-5995-1013-8
ISBN 13: 978-1-5995-1013-2

07 08 09 10 11 12 QWM 9 8 7 6 5 4 3 2

*In the eighteenth century, a generation fought
for America's independence from British rule.*

*In the nineteenth century, a generation fought to preserve
the Union from those who would tear it asunder.*

*In the twentieth century, a generation fought to
defend democracy from the forces of tyranny
and oppression in both Europe and the Pacific.*

*In the twenty-first century, a generation will fight for the
preservation and propagation of a culture based on truth.*

*This book is dedicated to that generation and
to the fulfillment of the legacy of its forefathers.*

CULTURALLY INCORRECT

contents

Introduction

Years ago, a missionary to India on furlough in the United States was traveling through the wheat fields of Kansas at harvest time. He was astounded to see the amber waves of grain that he had sung about as a schoolboy stretching to the horizon. As he stopped his car to take in the sight, a combine came into view, followed by another, and another, and yet another. As the great machines approached him rank upon rank, he was inspired to ask a question of one of the operators. He gained the man's attention as he drew near, and waved him to a halt. The farmer climbed down from the cab, took a red bandana from a pocket of his bibbed overalls and wiped the perspiration and wheat dust off his face.

"Sir," the missionary said, "I couldn't help but be stirred by the sight of your harvesting machinery. But today is Sunday. Aren't you ordinarily in church on Sunday?"

"Usually I am," the man replied. "But this isn't a usual circumstance. Last night we got the report that there is a storm to the west of us, and coming our way. We've got to go to work now, while there is time."

"Are all these machines yours?" asked the missionary.

"Oh, no," said the farmer, "these aren't all my combines. In fact, this isn't even my land. I live in the next township, and that's my neighbor from the next farm over, and that green one is from seven miles north, and that one is from the adjoining county, and there are one or two more I haven't even met, plus the fellow who farms this property. This is a good crop, but that storm will lay it flat if we don't get it in. You'll have to excuse me; I've got to get back to my work." The man climbed back in the cab of his great harvesting machine and roared off to complete his rounds through the waving wheat.

Fascinated, the missionary continued to watch as the huge combines raced to complete their task before the gathering storm released its fury on the standing grain. Soon the wind began to blow, reminding him that the storm was about to strike. He got back into his car and had only driven a short distance when the rain began to fall, first in drops, then in torrents, accompanied by fierce winds. Soon afterward, a chip of ice hit his windshield, then another, then another, then dozens, then hundreds, which then became thousands of hail stones which beat on his automobile with a continuous roar. At that moment he realized that the scene he was witnessing was a metaphor for what was about to transpire in our nation, represented to him by those waving fields of amber grain—there was a storm coming which was imminent and would be devastating if proper preparations were not made.

In 1858, a little-known candidate for the U.S. Senate named Abraham Lincoln scanned the cultural horizon of America and saw a fierce, gathering storm. With great courage, he pointed to that looming conflict even though, in the opinion of historians, doing so handed the election to his opponent, Stephen Douglas.

Standing before a thousand delegates and reporters in a sweltering Springfield, Illinois, assembly hall, Lincoln paraphrased the words of Jesus recorded in Matthew 12:25:

> A house divided against itself cannot stand. I believe this government cannot endure, permanently half slave and half free. I do not expect the Union to be dissolved—I do not expect the house to fall—but I do expect it will cease to be divided. It will become all one thing or all the other.

With prophetic clarity, Lincoln saw an imminent "war between the states"—one that would flow directly and unavoidably from the collision of competing visions for our nation; irreconcilable differences in values; and conflicting assumptions about the nature of man and his responsibilities to God. He rightly saw that one of those sets of visions and values must prevail; that you cannot steer a ship by two stars or a nation by two moral compasses.

I'm no Lincoln. I suppose the most conspicuous thing I have in common with that icon of American history—other than the fact that like Lincoln's, my feet stick out well past the edge of the typical hotel bed—is that we both grew up with roots in Kentucky, and our families both knew the challenges produced by poverty. But from my vantage point, I see something chillingly similar. Our national house is divided against itself once more—only this time, it's a war *within* the states.

Today, jagged fault lines scar our national landscape. Politically, culturally, morally, and spiritually we are a deeply divided people. The razor-thin margins in the presidential elections of 2000 and 2004 are but one manifestation of what has been called the "culture wars" and "the clash of cultures."

Lincoln took on the unpleasant task of sounding an alarm and calling like-minded men and women to battle and to sacrifice in a noble cause. I write today with a similar aim. You see, when worldviews collide, nations hang in the balance. So I must urge my friends to battle. Some who disagree with my point of view have misunderstood me and claimed that I am calling for armed conflict. I simply remind them of the words of the apostle Paul in 2 Corinthians 10:4–5: "For the weapons of our warfare are not carnal (fleshly) but mighty in God for pulling down strongholds, casting down arguments and every high thing that exalts itself against the knowledge of God, bringing every thought into captivity to the obedience of Christ . . ."

Notice that he emphasized thoughts as being crucial in this conflict. This battle is one of ideas, of thoughts, of mindsets, of **worldviews.**

Today our country is engaged in two wars: one abroad, and one at home.

The former is the conflict with a rabid Islamofascist ideology animated by global terrorism. The theater of battle is the whole world with flash points in Afghanistan, Iraq, Sudan, the Balkans, and the Philippines. Freedom, democracy, and economic progress for billions will depend upon the outcome of this battle. Western civilization is under siege.

Yet at this same pivotal moment in history, America also wrestles with herself—with just as much at stake. The minds and hearts of this generation have become the theater of conflict. It is a war of competing, mutually exclusive ways of viewing the universe and man's place in it. It is a clash of paradigms, of value systems, and of visions of the future.

Now, what has been simmering for decades has, in the last few years, come to a full boil. The election of George W. Bush in 2000 seems to have triggered a full-scale, multipronged cultural offensive aimed at removing, once and for all, traditional faith and morality from our laws, courts, schools, and marketplaces.

The people under siege are my fellow followers of Christ. Pundit and former talk show host, Dennis Miller, made this observation when I was a guest on his program: "The only people it's still okay to mock in this country are Christians." But in this case we find ourselves under attack from powerful forces *within* our nation. And, like America after the initial terrorist attacks on our nation in the nineties—the first World Trade Center bombing, the bombings of the U.S. embassies in Kenya and Tanzania, and the attack on the USS *Cole* in 2000—we seem dangerously slow to comprehend that, like it or not, we have a battle on our hands—a battle of ideas.

The question is, will we fight or slink passively into irrelevance and isolation? Will we simply sit by, horrified spectators, as our nation follows Europe's slide into a dark night of post-Christian paganism?

The great cathedrals of Europe where the Reformation was begun and the great tenets of the Christian faith were defended, have become museums—mere curiosities—relics of an irrelevant part of history. That is what America will look like in ten short years if we continue to pursue this path—like post-Christian Europe, we will be godless, faithless, rudderless, valueless; and without a seismic return to the discarded values of the past, hopeless.

As David Limbaugh wrote in his sobering book, *Persecution,* "Anti-Christian discrimination in our society is getting more blatant and more widespread every day."[1] In some cases, the viciousness of the attacks has been breathtaking. Stand-up comics, movies, and satirical sketches on cable television routinely hold America's believers up to the most withering scorn and mockery.

Isn't it ironic that the media and the academic elite hold "tolerance" and "diversity" above all virtues, and yet appear unwilling to tolerate anyone who dares to claim a belief in absolute right and wrong, the absolute sanctity of human life, the biblical definition of marriage, or a God who holds men accountable for their actions?

Such views are now deemed worse than politically incorrect. They have become, in fact, "Culturally Incorrect." This is ominous because culture runs deeper than politics—it goes to the very heart of who we are as a people. And this rising tide of intolerance for the cultural values that propelled our nation to greatness cannot be allowed to continue unchallenged.

That is why I write today. Because when worldviews collide, nations hang in the balance. So I must urge my friends to battle.

Yes, for a fleeting season following the September 11, 2001, attacks on our nation, we stood together, as we seem to do in times of great distress. For example, the students in Columbine High School prayed to God with reckless disregard for the separation of church and state or the wishes of the ACLU during the killing spree that shocked the entire nation; and we can all remember that the members of Congress stood together on the steps of the Capitol in Washington shortly after September 11, 2001 and sang *God Bless America.* But that thin veneer of unity after 9-11 was all too quickly worn away by the ongoing friction of cultural conflict. A brief flurry of flag waving and patriotic songs quickly subsided and was forgotten amid a rising din of name-calling and finger-pointing.

Please understand, I do not mention the global war on terror in order to demonize the "other side" or equate political or philosophical opponents with murderous terrorists. God knows we've seen and heard far too much of that in the last five or six years. Political correctness and cultural sensitivity constantly remind us we must certainly be cautious in an environment where quoting the Sunday school song, *Onward Christian Soldiers* causes some to recoil and hiss, "You want to start an armed holy war!"

The fact is, one can't pick up a newspaper, read an Internet "blog," or browse the current issues shelf at the local bookstore without finding decent people labeled as Big Fat Idiots, Morons, Lying Liars, Nazis, jihadists, and worse, simply because they hold opinions that run counter to the latest thinking in "enlightened" Hollywood circles or the better Upper West Side cocktail parties.

I personally have grown bone-weary of seeing "Bush=Hitler" signs at "progressive" political rallies, for such absurdly vicious comparisons do more than soil our national discourse—they dilute what should be an ongoing sense of horror and revulsion at what the twentieth century's dictators visited upon their fellow man, and what future Hitlers, Stalins, Maos, and Pol Pots will surely do in this new century if we are not vigilant.

Certainly, the majority of people on all sides of this clash of cultures are people of goodwill, good faith, and good intentions. But it is a war for the soul of our nation nonetheless. Not a war of our making. Not a war of our choosing. But a war forced upon us by those who would remake America from the foundations up. So I must urge my brothers and sisters to battle.

THE ROOTS OF
CULTURAL CONFLICT

So how did we get here? How did we get from the overwhelming national unity of World War II to the bitter, often vicious red state/blue state polarization? How is it that, in the twilight years of the Greatest Generation, the nation they fought heroically to preserve is now threatened to be rent asunder?

One reason is that in my parents' generation, 65 percent of Americans held Bible-based values. In my generation, that figure shrank to 35 percent. In my daughter's generation, at the current rate of erosion, that figure will only be 4 percent.[2]

In the pages that follow I hope to show you that the roots of this conflict run deep in our history and even predate our founding as a nation. At the birth of our nation—even as the framers and fathers hammered out our founding documents—two very distinct streams of philosophical thought wrestled for inclusion and dominance. In fact, these streams can be traced back through the centuries of human progress to the very Garden of Eden.

I'll show you how the antibiblical and now widely discredited ideas of men like Jean-Jacques Rousseau, Karl Marx, and Sigmund Freud still dominate our public discourse and policy making, while proven, time-tested truths are shouted down, censored, or labeled as "extremist" or simply "crazy."

For example, in February of 2005 HBO talk show host Bill Maher said the following on MSNBC's *Scarborough Country*:

> We are a nation that is unenlightened because of religion. I do believe that. I think that religion stops people from thinking. I think it justifies crazies. I think flying planes into a building was a faith-based initiative. I think religion is a neurological disorder.[3]

Maher went on to say:

> I don't hate America. I love America. I am just embarrassed that it has been taken over by people like evangelicals, by people who do not believe in science and rationality. It is the twenty-first century. And I will tell you, my friend. The future does not belong to the evangelicals. The future does not belong to religion.[4]

As you'll see in the following pages, Maher is not an isolated voice. He feels free to call faith a "neurological disorder" because it's rapidly becoming a key talking point for a massive coalition of secularists and rationalists who deeply resent the influence that people of faith still wield.

We'll see that Christianity and humanism have been on a collision course in our nation for more than a century. That the long-anticipated collision is now fully underway. And that, with the European branch of Western civilization in retreat and rapid collapse, it may be up to America to be the force for renewal, restoration, and defense of the ideals of the Reformation and the Great Awakening against their manifold attackers.

DEFENDING THE BULWARKS

Before I'm finished, we'll see that the key to that resistance lies in America's houses of worship and in the will to rise and fight that seems to lie dormant within the hearts of the believers who fill them—in other words, in the willingness to be culturally incorrect.

Two years ago, I wrote *Silent No More* as both a literary shot-across-the-bow of the dominant humanist culture and a wake-up call to a slumbering, lethargic, self-satisfied church. Since its publication, the battle lines have only sharpened and been joined. And yet large segments of Americans, even those who profess faith in Jesus Christ, sit idle still—in denial, self-absorption, bewilderment, or unwitting collaboration. Even so, the sporadic skirmishes of the 1980s and 1990s have given way to massive multipronged offensives that now threaten to overwhelm our crumbling bulwark traditions of decency, morality, honor, and goodness.

As Charles Colson has rightly written:

Turning our backs on the culture is a betrayal of our biblical mandate and our own heritage because it denies God's sovereignty over all of life. Nothing could be deadlier for the church or more ill-timed. To abandon the battlefield now is to desert the cause just when we are seeing the first signs that historic Christianity may be on the verge of a great breakthrough.[5]

He's right, so I will urge my brothers and sisters to battle: not a battle of violence and force, but of service and sacrifice; not of guns and missiles, but of truth and principle. For in this war we seek not to kill our enemies, but to win them. We seek not to find and imprison our opponents, but to liberate them. Terrorists operate by coercion. Christians have a different way of doing things—by persuasion, not by compulsion. As former Attorney General John Ashcroft has said, "It is against my religion to impose my religion."

What I hope to put forth here is more than just another rehash of how bad things have gotten and how outrageous the anti-Christian bigotry has grown in our country. Much more than that, I intend to call the church to nothing less than another Great Awakening.

The First Great Awakening was a watershed event in America, sweeping the colonies of the eastern seaboard and transforming the culture. Three centuries later, our nation unknowingly lives off the remnants of the spiritual capital amassed in that great moral movement. But that capital is running dangerously low.

With a heavy heart, I will demonstrate that much of the church's present impotence, compromise, and failure stems from a fundamental misunderstanding about what it really means to be a Christian. That the very gospel we preach is a mere shadow of the real thing. And that as a result, we have been a midwife to the births of entire generations of believers ill-equipped to engage the culture; unprepared for the rigors of the call of Christ; and unwilling to fight for their King.

And with compassion for those being ravaged by the false worldviews being preached in our universities and by the popular media culture, I will call my comrades to a full and vigorous engagement of the culture at every level.

During the dark, early days of World War II, Winston Churchill, in his first broadcast to the British people as prime minister, said, "Arm yourselves, and be ye men of valor, and be in readiness for the conflict; for it is better for us to perish in battle than to look upon the outrage of our nation and our altar."

I'm no Churchill. I'm just a preacher from the hills whom God rescued and redeemed, in the process granting me a platform from which to speak to my fellow saints and fellow citizens. But a knowing burns in the depths of my soul—a knowing that a similar call to sacrifice and service needs to be made to my brothers and sisters in this hour of history. So on the pages that follow I will sound that call.

There is a price we must pay to rescue a generation, restore a nation, and revitalize a civilization. I must remind you that self-sacrifice is entry level Christianity. The question is, are we willing to pay that price? If we are, then we must understand our opponents—those well-meaning people who would dismantle the Christian worldview that has been the structural paradigm of our amazing society, replacing it with one that cannot possibly stand under the weight of human frailty and weakness.

We must understand those we are trying to persuade. So on the pages that follow, I will do more than point to the ways in which humanists, secularists, and neo-pagans have launched a full-scale assault on the values and virtues upon which our nation and culture were built. I'll show you *why* they think it's the right thing to do.

You see, actions follow assumptions. Positions, behaviors, and even voting patterns are downstream. *Follow that stream to its headwaters and you'll find a worldview.*

Make no mistake, many on the other side hate us and despise everything we stand for. But regardless, our biblical mandate is to love and bless in return. Challenge them? Yes. Argue for the superiority and accuracy of our worldview? We must. You see, when worldviews collide, nations hang in the balance. So I will urge my brothers and sisters to engage, to lead, to influence. And I'll lay out a strategy for cultural victory.

part one

WHEN WORLDS COLLIDE

On a mid-December day in 1944, three powerful German armies plunge into the heavily-forested Ardennes region of eastern Belgium and northern Luxembourg. Their goal is to reach the sea, trap four allied armies, and reverse the momentum of the war.

Thinking the Ardennes Forest is the least likely spot for a German offensive, American Staff Commanders have chosen to keep the line thin, in order to concentrate manpower on expected attacks north and south of the Ardennes.

America's 106th Infantry Division, in place on a finger of territory jutting out into Germany, is hit with full force. After three days of battle, two of the Regiments, the 422nd and the 423rd, are surrounded.

The Battle of the Bulge is underway. And the fate of Europe turns on the outcome.

(JOHN KLINE, *HISTORY OF THE 106TH INFANTRY DIVISION-WWII*)[1]

one

SURVEYING THE BATTLEFIELD

Surveys may not be glamorous, but they are necessary to determine where we are and where we need to go. In this chapter I will point out that something is going deeply and dangerously wrong in our nation. But I suspect you already knew that.

If you have a television, Internet access, or simply a functioning set of eyes and ears, you are acutely aware that our culture is dancing on a slippery slope of amoral madness—blindfolded. You have watched the entertainment industry relentlessly push and extend the boundaries of decency, knowing that outrageousness is the surest road to wealth and fame today.

You have seen wrong upheld as right. You have seen right denounced as intolerance. You have watched efforts to redefine the terms *marriage* and *family* into meaninglessness meet with increasing success. And you have seen an all-out effort to push faith to the outer fringes of our national life.

You know something is very wrong. But before we go further it's important that you fully comprehend where we stand. You need to know what is at stake. It is vital that you know the national price we will pay if you and I sit idly by and do nothing. Yet I also want you to see that there is real cause to be hopeful. I want you to know there are some clear pathways back to sanity and wholeness before us.

In fact, our current situation reminds me of the opening lines of Charles Dickens's *A Tale of Two Cities*—"It was the best of times, it was the worst of times, it was the age of wisdom, it was the age of foolishness . . . it was the season of Light, it was the season of Darkness."[1]

On the one hand, a huge majority of Americans today claim to believe in God—nearly 90 percent! And a full 40 percent profess beliefs that indicate they are born-again children of God.[2] And yet precious few of those Christians actually live lives that are markedly different from those who do not claim the name of Christ. It's not the atheist shaking his fist toward the heavens that is a threat to Christianity; but far more dangerous is the so-called Christian, who despite his outward appearance, is a verifiable stranger to the character of the Christ he claims to serve.

When you observe the behaviors, values, and dysfunctions of the average "Christian" family, you don't come away with a sense that these are people who believe there is anything beyond this present life or that one day we will all stand before a Judge who will weigh our thoughts and deeds.

Today, Christians can be found in the highest levels of government, at the helms of Fortune 500 companies, and increasingly, even among the ranks of Hollywood actors, writers, and producers. At the same time, we are witnessing an all-out campaign to de-legitimize and stigmatize Christian belief and even criminalize the proclamation of biblical truth. Indeed, we are not many steps away from having the public reading of certain Scriptures declared a "hate crime."[3]

A Swedish pastor was sentenced to one month in prison for reading Scriptures regarding homosexuality, although his conviction was later overturned by the Swedish Supreme Court.[4] Canada has passed hate crime legislation which loosely defines what constitutes hate speech, leaving it open for interpretation by the courts. More than a few observers say the effect of this legislation will be to inhibit any public discourse, such as preaching, that may be regarded as unfavorable to homosexuals or other protected groups. California passed a similar law, called the Omnibus Hate Crimes Act of 2004.

Through television, gospel preaching and teaching are more widely available than at any time in our history. Yet at the same time television programming is becoming increasingly vile, violent, and valueless. Witness the fact that some of the most celebrated shows on television have been HBO offerings like *The Sopranos* or *Sex and the City*, network hits like *Desperate Housewives*, and syndicated perennials like *The Jerry Springer Show*.

A random, five-minute sampling of *The Sopranos*, for example, will expose you to more profanity than a typical sailor hears in a day. The steady drumbeat of "*f*" words that forms the soundtrack for the program is laid over images of graphic violence and sex.

On those too-rare occasions when the entertainment industry provides something wholesome and family-friendly, it tends to be a huge success. There is a tremendous, unsatisfied hunger in our nation for entertainment that is clean and uplifting. The recent successes of *The Chronicles of Narnia* in theaters, and television programs like *Extreme Makeover: Home Edition* are evidence of this demand. In fact, a study by the Christian Film and Television Commission showed that seven of the top ten box offices successes of 2005 contained no sexual content. The commission also reported that family-friendly films as a group consistently do best at the box office.[5]

Meanwhile, Howard Stern and ten thousand imitators grow spectacularly wealthy feeding America's appetite for the seedy and seamy.

Stern is a fifty-something-year-old man who has built a wildly successful radio career out of talking like a sex-obsessed thirteen-year-old boy. After repeatedly being fined by the Federal Communications Commission for violating decency standards, Stern recently made the jump to satellite radio. Why? Because it is unregulated—giving him the freedom to be as vile and perverse as he wishes. In making the move, Stern claimed he was striking a blow for free speech. He apparently was also striking a blow for free enterprise. His deal with Sirius satellite radio will pay him $500 million over five years.

Yes, Jesus-honoring self-help books like *The Purpose-Driven Life* and *Your Best Life Now* are featured on the *New York Times* best-seller lists for months at a time. But at the very same time, Dan Brown's *The Da Vinci Code*—a novel that claims to be based upon "facts" and suggests that Jesus of Nazareth survived the cross and fathered a child by Mary Magdalene—has become one of the greatest fiction success stories of the new millennium.

OUR "BATTLE OF THE BULGE"

Clearly, we are standing at a decisive moment. It is a moment very much like the Battle of the Bulge I referenced at the opening of this section. Allow me to remind you of the context of that pivotal chapter in history. (And for heaven's sake, don't check out on me here just because I'm about to review a little history. This is exciting stuff! They've made movies out of this!) First, some background.

Beginning with the invasion of Poland in 1939, Nazi Germany had marched unchecked through most of the continent of Europe. By 1941, the Axis armies of Germany, Austria, and Italy had overrun Czechoslovakia, Belgium, Denmark, Sweden, the Netherlands, and France. Their only setback had come at the hands of Churchill's tenacious Britain when Hitler's ferocious bombing campaign of England failed to adequately soften the nation's defenses and infrastructure enough to allow an invasion of the British Isles.

Nevertheless, Hitler and his Axis allies seemed well on their way to achieving the world domination for which they believed they were destined.

Then, the Japanese attack on Pearl Harbor on December 7, 1941, finally brought the United States into the war. Gradually, and at tremendous cost, the tide began to turn. The forward momentum of the Axis powers was stopped.

But the Allies still needed to take back the territory lost on the continent of Europe. Thus, in 1944, American and British forces successfully invaded Italy at Anzio. It was followed five months later by the D-Day invasion at the beaches of Normandy, France. This invasion was depicted with horrifying accuracy by Steven Spielberg in his film *Saving Private Ryan.*

Using the hard-won beachhead established at Normandy, the Allies began the slow, bloody work of pushing the Axis powers out of France —one village and farm at a time. By August 25, 1944, Paris was liberated. By December, the Allies were in position to invade Germany herself. Thus, for the very first time in the long war, German armies faced the real prospect of having to fight to defend their own homeland.

This brings us to that ferocious German counteroffensive I described at the opening of this section and why, in my opinion, it mirrors the current phase of the "culture wars."

For most of the last century, the forces of secularism and humanism enjoyed victory after victory. One by one, the primary institutions of our society fell to these philosophies.

Take the arts, for example. In the 1800s you had the great American painters of the Hudson River School creating majestic landscapes that they very consciously saw as reflections of God's glory manifest in His creation. Just a few decades later, we find Jackson Pollock randomly slinging paint at a large canvas and being celebrated as a genius. As we'll see in a later chapter, this steady degrading of art from meticulous and beautiful to random and chaotic was a direct outgrowth of the culture's embrace of Darwin's new evolutionary gospel of random chance.

We also lost the universities. Many of the most prestigious universities in America were founded by Christian men as distinctly Christian institutions. Harvard was founded in 1636 so the Puritans of the Massachusetts colony could train their own preachers and not have to depend on Oxford and Cambridge in England. Princeton was established by the "New Light" Presbyterians and was originally intended to train Presbyterian ministers. Ten Congregationalist ministers pooled their personal book collections to form Yale University's first library. Most of the other Ivy League schools were likewise founded by Christian people with sacred aims.

How is it, then, that today, the massive majority of our institutions of higher learning are not only blatantly humanist and atheist in their orientation, but they are fiercely intolerant of the ideas that energized their founders?

Finally, the government itself—particularly the judicial branch of government—became dominated by those who reject the truth of the Bible and much of the Judeo-Christian framework upon which our nation had been founded and had flourished. As I pointed out in my earlier book, *Silent No More*, the last few decades of the twentieth century brought us a series of disastrous U.S. Supreme Court rulings that turned the Constitution's "freedom of religion" provision on its head:

> So now we live in a society in which atheists file lawsuits to have "In God We Trust" erased from our money, in which the American Civil Liberties Union (ACLU) challenges almost every expression of our Christian heritage, and in which "faith-based initiatives"—of a kind our Founding Fathers enacted themselves—are considered by some legal minds to be a violation of the law. Simply put, we are watching the banishment of our heritage.[6]

At the same time, the great mainline denominations that had played such a key role in the early greatness of our nation began to abandon their biblical roots and become more theologically—and as a direct result, more politically—liberal. They began a progressive embrace of much of the humanist agenda and thought. And as they did, they began a steady slide into irrelevance and extinction.

In the twenty-five-year period between 1965 and 1990, America's historic Protestant churches lost from one-fifth to one-third of their members. As writers for the scholarly journal *First Things* noted back in the 1990s:

> America's so-called mainline Protestant churches aren't what they used to be. For generations on end, the Methodists, Presbyterians, Congregationalists, Episcopalians, and kindred denominations

reported net annual membership gains. But in the early 1960s their growth slowed down, and after the middle of the decade they had begun to lose members. With very few exceptions, the decline has continued to this date.[7]

Throughout the 1940s, 1950s, and 1960s, traditional Christianity seemed to be in full retreat. So much so, that many of the proponents of the more "enlightened" ideologies began to foresee a glorious day in which America would be freed from the last vestiges of this primitive and restrictive belief system.

For example, by 1973 Gloria Steinem felt optimistic enough to write, "By the year 2000 we will, I hope, raise our children to believe in human potential, not God."[8] That same year, many of the nation's political, academic, and cultural elites signed a document called the Humanist Manifesto II. Among its numerous confident declarations was, "No deity will save us, we must save ourselves. Promises of immortal salvation or fear of eternal damnation are both illusory and harmful."[9]

That was also the year in which comedian George Carlin would get big laughs by saying, "I would never want to be a member of a group whose symbol was a guy nailed to two pieces of wood."

But as the apostle Paul reminds us in Romans 5:20, where sin abounds, grace abounds all the more. The late 1960s and early 1970s saw the emergence of the Jesus Movement and a remarkable wave of charismatic renewal in many churches. While many of the older mainline denominations continued their slide into obscurity, churches that remained faithful to the message and authority of the Bible—the Assemblies of God and the Southern Baptists to name two—thrived. At the same time, nondenominational churches, meetings, and gatherings began springing up by the thousands all over America, drawing millions as they proclaimed (and demonstrated) the ongoing relevance of God's Word for wholeness, fulfillment, and successful living.

One of my fondest memories from this period was a national youth event I attended at Houston's Astrodome, where I was one of tens of thousands of young people from all across the country who came by car, bus, train, and plane to participate in worship, teaching, and evangelism for several days. I remember staying in an unfinished apartment complex, sleeping on the floor, eating cereal out of an economy box, learning The Four Spiritual Laws, sharing my faith door to door, celebrating with others who loved Jesus as much as me, and generally having the time of my life.

Then, in 1980, Ronald Reagan was sent to the White House. From the standpoint of the cultural Left, his election was unthinkable and appalling. Reagan was the antithesis of everything they believed and stood for. But in 1980 they had every reason to believe Reagan was just an anomaly—a temporary, nostalgic, God-and-country detour on America's steady march to humanist utopia. But that belief was wrong. From my point of view, Ronald Reagan restored some things in America that were becoming endangered—hope, for one thing; along with a sense of national pride and patriotism, and a determination to overcome the challenges of the age and to restore faith in a nation that desperately needed renewal.

America wasn't ready to follow Europe's example and go quietly into a post-Christian night. Well underneath the radar of the cultural elites, a movement toward faith and values, not away from them, was well underway.

So just as the Axis armies had seen the Allies reverse many of the territorial gains they had made so quickly, so have the forces of secularism and humanism seen their monopolistic hold on the culture slipping away.

This has produced the fierce "push back" we are now witnessing in this struggle for the soul of our nation.

The close and bitterly contested election of George W. Bush in 2000 seemed to trigger something ferocious and desperate among America's ruling cultural elite. A viciousness that emerged only occasionally in the Reagan years became standard operating procedure almost overnight. This was more than just the usual hurly-burly of politics. There was clearly a spiritual element to this hatred. You'll recall that during the presidential primaries, George W. Bush created quite a stir when he was asked during a debate which historical figure had the greatest impact on him. His now-famous answer was: "Jesus Christ, because He changed my heart."

I can tell you from experience that He will change yours, too! That's what He does—that's why He came; born in a barn because that's where a lamb ought to be born . . . this I know to be true. God changes lives—He changed mine at eight years of age in a cinder block building with wooden pews and 40 watt light bulbs—because we couldn't afford 100 watt bulbs. The forgiveness of God washed me as clean inside as my mother's homemade lye soap did on the outside.

Why was George W. Bush's statement different than, say, Reagan's frequent references to God? Because the dominant leftist culture assumed Ronald Reagan only *pretended* to be a Christian to dupe the backward, religious rubes in "flyover country"—their derisive term for the heartland of America lying between the two "progressive and enlightened" coasts. But from their perspective, George W. Bush *was* one of the religious rubes from flyover country. And it was more than they could bear.

Ambiguously talking about "God" was one thing. Openly and unashamedly using the *J* word was something else entirely.

Of course, as many of the personal letters and papers that have come to light since his death have shown, Ronald Reagan was, indeed, a deeply spiritual man who had a real relationship with Christ and a firm grasp of the biblical view of man, God, and history. The letters of the man whom Lyndon Johnson's former secretary of defense, Clark Clifford, sneeringly described as "an amiable dunce" actually reveal an impressive command of sophisticated arguments by thinkers such as John Locke and C. S. Lewis.

But again, the secularists thought Reagan's frequent references to faith were all theatrics. "After all, hadn't he been an actor for all those years?" No, it was President Bush's unmistakable, unapologetic faith that really sent the cultural elites over the edge. And thus, in early 2001, once the bitterly contested election results were finally decided, the cultural counterattack started in earnest and our "battle of the bulge" began. That counterattack was swift, fierce, and multipronged. Within weeks of the election, MTV launched a despicable comedy series called *That's My Bush!* In it, a character who was clearly meant to represent President Bush was portrayed as a stupid, hard-drinking, drug-taking, southern Christian hypocrite.

Immediately, stand-up comics on late night television began mocking the president's faith and the spiritual motivations of many who supported him. Dozens of books designed to validate and reinforce the biased assumptions of the Bush-haters were rushed into print.

Liberal columnist Molly Ivins, who, because of her Texas roots, was a seasoned Bush-hater before Bush-hating was fashionable, got in early with *Shrub: The Short but Happy Political Life of George W. Bush,* and it was followed by dozens of others. On the whole, these books were not created to persuade the undecided or enlighten the uninformed. They were raw red meat for those who had already made up their minds. They were fuel on a fire that was already burning hot and wild.

Then there was MoveOn.org—a Web-based, left-wing, grassroots fund-raising machine formed during the Clinton-Lewinsky scandal and the subsequent investigation by special prosecutor Kenneth Starr. The name of the organization came from their contention that the country and Congress should stop being occupied by whether or not President Clinton lied under oath about this or that—and should just "move on." At that time, the movement's founders claimed they were concerned about the level of "partisan warfare in Washington." But with the election of George W. Bush, the organization found a new purpose. It quickly became a powerful force for ratcheting up the partisan warfare to the highest possible level.

In the yearlong run-up to the 2004 elections, MoveOn.org published television spots comparing George W. Bush to Adolph Hitler. One spot featured archival footage of Hitler speaking to a cheering crowd. As fake subtitles of the translation appeared on the bottom of the screen, Hitler gradually morphed into Bush. The subtitles had Hitler-Bush saying:

"We have taken new measures to protect our homeland, I believe I am acting in accordance with the will of the Almighty Creator, God told me to strike at al-Qaeda and I struck them, and then He instructed me to strike at Saddam, which I did."

Such scaremongering about faith wasn't focused solely on the president. Because a number of his key advisors and cabinet members were evangelical Christians, they were targets as well. Attorney General John Ashcroft was the particular focus of astonishingly harsh and personal attacks because of his faith.

On January 16, 2001, at the height of Ashcroft's Senate confirmation hearings, ABC newsman Peter Jennings led his evening newscast with this question: "Do John Ashcroft's strong evangelical beliefs disqualify him from holding an important position on the new president's cabinet?"[10]

Jennings wasn't alone in posing that loaded question. Throughout the process, pundits and critics across the country either implied or outright declared that someone who takes the Bible seriously had no business holding high office in our enlightened, pluralistic new millennium.

Such attacks increased all the more when it later became known that a number of voluntary Bible studies were being held in the Justice Department building before working hours. At that point, the secularists were utterly convinced that their worst fears had been made manifest. The "pod-people" had taken over the government! Iranian-style theocracy in America couldn't be far behind.

The venomous rhetoric and attacks continued to escalate right up through the presidential election of 2004. Those who were horrified by the president's faith-based approach to domestic policy and his muscular prosecution of the war on terror pulled out all the stops to see that George W. Bush followed his father's path as a one-term president.

Thus in the year preceding the election we saw the release of Michael Moore's outrageously deceptive "documentary," *Fahrenheit*

911, accompanied by full promotional cooperation of the mainstream media. MoveOn.org did its part by mobilizing its massive database in support of the film.

Far Left billionaires like George Soros poured fortunes in the form of "soft money" into groups like MoveOn.org that could be counted on to work against Bush's reelection. As a story in the *Washington Post* reported a full year before the election:

> George Soros, one of the world's richest men, has given away nearly $5 billion to promote democracy in the former Soviet bloc, Africa and Asia. Now he has a new project: defeating President Bush. "It is the central focus of my life," Soros said, his blue eyes settled on an unseen target. The 2004 presidential race, he said in an interview, is "a matter of life and death."[11]

Soros eventually poured an estimated $30 million into organizations that could and would smear the president.

At the same time, anti-Bush books flooded the market and received maximum promotional exposure in the mainstream media. Titles released in the twelve months prior to the election included:

The Bush Haters Handbook: An A-Z Guide to the Most Appalling Presidency of the Past 100 Years
The Family: The Real Story of the Bush Dynasty
American Dynasty: Worse Than Watergate
Lies and the Lying Liars Who Tell Them
Bushwhacked: Life in George W. Bush's America
Stupid White Men . . . and Other Sorry Excuses for the State of the Nation!
Taking Back America: And Taking Down the Radical Right
The Book on Bush: How George W. (Mis)leads America
Worse Than Watergate: The Secret Presidency of George W. Bush
The Price of Loyalty: George W. Bush, the White House, and the Education of Paul O'Neill

*Fraud: The Strategy Behind the Bush Lies and Why the Media
    Didn't Tell You*
Cruel and Unusual: Bush/Cheney's New World Order
Had Enough? A Handbook for Fighting Back
The Lies of George W. Bush: Mastering the Politics of Deception
*Thieves in High Places: They've Stolen Our Country—and It's Time
    to Take It Back*
The Great Unraveling: Losing Our Way in the New Century

Never in U.S. electoral history had so much publishing firepower
been concentrated on the destruction of a single candidate. The
authors of these books were granted wide open access to other media
streams to promote their books and their negative views of the president. Major television news programs, such as *The Today Show* and
Good Morning America, welcomed the authors and lobbed softball
questions at them. The *New York Times, Washington Post, Los Angeles
Times,* and other major papers could be counted on for glowing
reviews and frequent mentions.

Meanwhile, a book critical of the president's challenger,[12] John Kerry,
written by veterans who served with Kerry in Vietnam, was either condemned or simply ignored—mostly the latter. On the few occasions
the authors were interviewed, they were grilled aggressively and forced
to spend the time defending their motives and their integrity.

In years past, a major political party would have kept a controversial extremist like Michael Moore at arm's length. But not in 2004.
Desperate times call for desperate measures. So at the Democratic
National Convention in Boston, Moore was given VIP treatment and
even sat with former President Jimmy Carter in his private box.

Hollywood did its best to use America's cult of celebrity to rally the
troops. Liberal activist-actor Alec Baldwin promised to move out of
the country if Bush won reelection. (At this writing he is still enjoying
the blessings of U.S. residency.) Likewise, Hollywood director Robert
Altman threatened to move to France if Kerry didn't get elected.

Hollywood has-beens and current entertainment celebrities alike became noted philosophers and constitutional scholars on the talk show circuit. Cameron Diaz went on Oprah Winfrey's show to urge her sisters to vote. With Drew Barrymore and Christina Aguilera nodding in approval, she pronounced:

> We have a voice now, and we're not using it, and women have so much to lose. I mean, we could lose the right to our bodies. We could lose . . . if you think that rape should be legal, then don't vote. But if you think that you have a right to your body, and you have a right to say what happens to you and fight off that danger of losing that, then you should vote.[13]

As the election moved into the home stretch, polls indicated that the result was too close to call. The steady media drumbeat of anti-Bush news and rhetoric was not having the desired result. The desperation of the cultural establishment grew.

However, the Left had learned a valuable lesson in the power of negative news during the presidential election of 2000. One week prior to that election, most polls showed Texas governor George W. Bush with a significant lead over his opponent, Vice President Al Gore. But just a few days before the election, news agencies broke a story about Bush having been arrested for "driving under the influence" years earlier. Though the information came from a prominent Democratic activist in Maine, the story received the widest possible coverage. The Bush organization had to spend the final days of the campaign answering embarrassing questions rather than talking about issues.

Many political analysts credit that eleventh hour story with the sudden, last-minute tightening of the race in the polls. A few days later Gore actually received a slim majority of the popular vote, though he lost the Electoral College.

If an eleventh-hour bombshell could wipe out a commanding lead overnight in 2000, why wouldn't it swing a neck-and-neck race in 2004? Thus, just weeks before the election, Dan Rather used a *60 Minutes* television segment to announce the "discovery" of a damning memo from the records of the Texas Air National Guard—a document that seemed to prove that Bush had shirked his duty as a guardsman. But within hours of the broadcast, savvy Internet bloggers quickly and persuasively showed the documents to be a crude forgery. As before, the source of the memo turned out to be a longtime liberal Democratic activist.

As you know, Bush was reelected. And to the deep consternation of the cultural elites, a lot of the post-election analysis pointed to the involvement of evangelical Christians on the behalf of Bush as being a key factor in his victory.

As I said in my book *Silent No More*,

"I canceled my fall schedule to tour cities in America on a *Silent No More* tour. In sixteen meetings within thirty days, I spoke across the country, and especially in my home state of Ohio, making the case for moral values to as many people as would listen . . . .

"The tour was an eye-opening experience for me and, it seemed, for those attending. In congregation after congregation, as I talked about the terrible toll same-sex marriage would inflict on our culture, I saw facial expressions change. It was as though scales had fallen from their eyes, and they could finally see the cost of sitting on the sidelines while the political process went forward without them . . . .

"Evangelical Christians not only turned out to the polls in large numbers, but they also overwhelmingly supported the candidates and issues that best reflected their values. According to the Barna Group, although evangelicals were just 7 percent of the voting-age population, they constituted 11 percent of the voters."[14]

This, of course, only further inflamed the forces that regard Bible-centric believers as the principal obstacle to what they view as progress.

Their frustration was perfectly captured by a cartoon map that quickly began to circulate on the Internet right after the election. The map showed the northern and west coast "blue states," which had been carried by John Kerry, as having joined Canada to form "The United States of Canada." Bush's "red states" had been relabeled as well: "Jesusland."

THE ANTI-CHRISTIAN STRATEGY

Now the forces of secularism and humanism had identified their true enemy. In their view, Republicans or even political conservatives weren't really the problem—Christians and Christianity were. Hence the battle in which we find ourselves locked today. An all-out effort is underway to roll back the modest but encouraging gains that Christians have made in recent years.

What quickly emerged after the 2004 elections was a dual strategy for dealing with Christianity's growing influence—the goal is to either demonize or demoralize.

The demonization began even before the election results were in. One noteworthy example is an essay by former Clinton administration Labor Secretary Robert Reich in the magazine *The American Prospect*. In the article, titled "Bush's God," Reich lumps America's Christians together with rabid Islamic extremists and terrorists, but actually seems to believe that little old Pentecostal grandmothers are the greater threat of the two. He wrote,

> The great conflict of the twenty-first century will not be between the West and terrorism. Terrorism is a tactic, not a belief. The true battle will be between modern civilization and anti-modernists; between those who believe in the primacy of the individual and those who believe that human beings owe their allegiance and identity to a higher authority; between those who give priority to life in this world and those who believe that human life is mere preparation for an existence beyond life; between those who believe in science, reason, and logic and those who believe that truth is revealed through Scripture

and religious dogma. Terrorism will disrupt and destroy lives. But terrorism itself is not the greatest danger we face.[15]

With startling candor, Reich states plainly what many others on the Left clearly think, but never dare to say—namely, that Bible-believing Christians are no different than militant jihadists blindly following the latest *fatwa* handed down by the mullahs. Of course, in their minds the Christians are a more imminent threat because of their numbers and influence in America.

I may not have been convinced of this myself until I had an experience that proved it to me beyond any doubt. In January of 2006, a group of thirty-one predominantly liberal clergy released a statement that they had filed a complaint with the Internal Revenue Service against two of the ministries under my leadership, World Harvest Church and Reformation Ohio. They did not call or contact me about any of their concerns before releasing this statement, nor did they list their names. When asked why they chose to remain anonymous, they stated that they were fearful of my response.

I was astonished beyond measure for two reasons. First, it was amazing to me that clergy would take a matter with another clergyman in the same community public without attempting to resolve the matter through personal communication. Next, I was incredulous that they would feel fearful about my intentions toward them after having filed such a complaint.

When I responded to their allegations, I said, "They are brothers. We will embrace them as brothers . . . we'll unleash the troops to pray for them." The context of that statement was to pray for them in accordance with Jesus' words in Matthew 5:44: "But I say to you, love your enemies, bless those who curse you, do good to those who hate you, and pray for those who spitefully use you and persecute you."

I have never heard the first word of encouragement from these clergymen or their organizations toward our efforts to feed the hungry, clothe the naked, or free those in bondage. No wonder churches are having difficulty focusing on the goal of winning the world!

Reich is not the only one trying to tar Christians with the terrorist brush. It has actually become a major talking point in the demonization part of the strategy. In a September 2004 interview with *The New Yorker* magazine, former Vice President Al Gore had this to say about the faith of George W. Bush: "It's a particular kind of religiosity. It's the American version of the same fundamentalist impulse that we see in Saudi Arabia, in Kashmir, in religions around the world: Hindu, Jewish, Christian and Muslim."[16]

Columnist Don Feder rightly bristled at Gore's smear of believers. His response is worth citing at length:

> When he speaks of a "fundamentalist impulse" in Christianity, Gore is also degrading and demonizing evangelical Christians. The term fundamentalist implies fanaticism . . . When the left says fundamentalist it means—"takes religion seriously, believes in the Bible literally, thinks The Ten Commandments are more than suggestions, disagrees with the ACLU on abortion and gay marriage": in other words, miscreants, mutants, degenerates and the criminally insane— the sort of folks who would never get a grant from The Heinz Family Foundation.
>
> Liberals in the news media sneer at "fundamentalists" (the left's code word for evangelicals) as ignorant bigots. Liberals in Hollywood caricature them (by portraying born-again Christians as trailer-park trash with room-temperature IQs, or Savonarola wannabes). Liberals in politics smear Bible-believing Christians by comparing them to the religion of holy war and suicide bombers.
>
> As Gore does here, by speaking of Christians like the president in the same breath as Saudi Arabia and the Kashmir—where Moslems on steroids shoot, bomb, and behead infidels, the clear implication is that fundamentalists/evangelicals are the American equivalent of suicide bombers.[17]

And as blogger and radio host Hugh Hewitt wrote in an article for *World Magazine*: "'Loonies,' 'The American Taliban,' 'Frist's Jihadists,' 'the Ayatollah bin Dobson'—all these terms and more were thrown at evangelical Christians last week . . . Many media and political circles are showing a rise in Christian-bashing."[18]

This expanding program of making people of faith out to be dangerous fanatics is well underway on both sides of the Atlantic. For example, in January 2006, the outspoken British scientist and evolutionist Richard Dawkins hosted a television special titled *The Virus of Faith*. In it he compared Moses to Hitler and labeled the New Testament "a sado-masochistic doctrine." But he saved some of his choicest rhetoric for Christian parents, calling the teaching of religion to children "child abuse." Dawkins proclaimed:

> Innocent children are being saddled with demonstrable falsehoods. It's time to question the abuse of childhood innocence with superstitious ideas of hellfire and damnation. Isn't it weird the way we automatically label a tiny child with its parents' religion?[19]

Let me attempt to put this in proper perspective. In a culture with 65 percent of adults who espoused moral values which were biblically based, such a declaration would be dismissed without serious consideration. But today, with only 35 percent of adults professing those same values, these comments are taken seriously. When only 4 percent of adults hold to moral values, they will very likely be considered more true than the Bible itself.

Dawkins went on to assert that Christian schools have been "deeply damaging" to generations of children. I could not disagree more. It is no secret to anyone who cares to examine the record of public education in America that it has failed, is failing, and will continue to fail if we refuse to undertake a total overhaul of a broken and corrupt system. The decline and fall of public education has been accelerated by the continual erosion of any vestige of biblical values in the public school classroom.

To the degree that Christians can't be demonized, they must be demoralized. Thus, while whole segments of the dominant humanist culture are busy bashing evangelicals in the hopes of making them cultural pariahs, a growing cadre of scientific "rationalists" hopes to demoralize believers by undermining their confidence in their faith.

Zoologist Richard Dawkins, mentioned above, is just one member of a growing group of militant, atheist intellectuals on a crusade to demonstrate that the Christian faith is false.

One example is the recent documentary movie titled *The God Who Wasn't There*. It is a film that aims to prove not that the Bible's claims about Jesus aren't wholly accurate, but that Jesus never existed at all! The promotional Web site for the movie tells us:

In this provocative, critically acclaimed documentary, you will discover that:

- The early founders of Christianity seem wholly unaware of the idea of a human Jesus.
- The Jesus of the Gospels bears a striking resemblance to other ancient heroes and the figureheads of pagan savior cults.
- Contemporary Christians are largely ignorant of the origins of their religion.
- Fundamentalism is as strong today as it ever has been, with an alarming 44 percent of Americans believing Jesus will return to earth in their lifetimes.
- And God simply isn't there.[20]

The God Who Wasn't There was a big hit in art houses and on college campuses around the country. It is now out on DVD, and atheist activist groups are encouraging members to pass copies along to any weak and wavering Christians they know or to host parties in which groups of friends are invited over to view the documentary.

Featured prominently in the film is Sam Harris, a Stanford graduate with a degree in philosophy. Harris has written a book titled *The End of Faith: Religion, Terror and the Future of Reason,* which claims to deliver "a startling analysis of the clash of faith and reason in the modern world" and to provide "a harrowing glimpse of mankind's willingness to suspend reason in favor of religious beliefs, even when these beliefs inspire the worst of human atrocities."

Concerning *The End of Faith*, an admiring reviewer at the hyper-liberal British newspaper, *The Observer,* called the book "a radical attack on the most sacred of liberal precepts—the notion of tolerance" and "an eminently sensible rallying cry for a more ruthless secularization of society."[21]

What an apt description of what we are now facing! A ruthless secularization of our society is precisely what is being attempted. And a major component of the effort involves the use of dubious science to undermine our faith and delegitimize our convictions.

For example, a 2004 book by genetic researcher Dean Hamer caused a major buzz in the general press and received wide national attention. In *The God Gene: How Faith Is Hardwired into Our Genes*, Hamer speculates that a series of genetic mutations actually cause us to be religiously oriented and to seek God.[22] Hamer drew heavily from an earlier collection of essays and papers published as *NeuroTheology: Brain, Science, Spirituality, Religious Experience* as well as *The Mystical Mind: Probing the Biology of Religious Experience; Why God Won't Go Away: Brain Science and the Biology of Belief;* and *Religion Explained: The Evolutionary Origins of Religious Thought.*

Atheist activists immediately seized on the hypothesis and trumpeted it as additional proof that everything in the universe has a natural, material explanation. "See there," they said, "your spiritual experiences and encounters with God are nothing more than a series of chemical reactions."

But even the scientific community was skeptical. A review of Hamer's book in *Scientific American* magazine stated:

Whatever you want to call it, this is a frustrating book. The role that genes play in religion is a fascinating question that's ripe for the asking. Psychologists, neurologists and even evolutionary biologists have offered insights about how spiritual behaviors and beliefs emerge from the brain. It is reasonable to ask, as Hamer does, whether certain genes play a significant role in faith. **But he is a long way from providing an answer.**[23] (emphasis added)

The high hopes of the atheist activists notwithstanding, no Christian should find this research troubling or problematic in any way. The fact is, if they find incontrovertible proof tomorrow that we are born hardwired to seek God and to want to know Him, it will just be additional evidence of intelligent design.

More than 350 years ago Christian mathematician Blaise Pascal said we all have a "God-shaped void" inside us. Three thousand years ago King Solomon observed that God had "put eternity" in the hearts of men (Ecclesiastes 3:11).

Nevertheless, in the war of ideas currently being waged in our culture, there are those who would use science and reason as a club with which to pummel evangelical Christians into silence or surrender. Yet as we'll see in Chapter 6, scientific inquiry and biblical truth are not inherently at odds. In fact, Judeo-Christian monotheism actually made modern science possible!

Nevertheless, we are in the midst of our very own Battle of the Bulge. Much is at stake. Our lines *must* hold. Because, as we're about to see, our needed reinforcements may not be ready to fight.

THE DOCTOR IS SICK

As I stated in the Introduction, our nation's God-given destiny hangs on the outcome of the current cultural battle we are fighting.

Today powerful forces would push the United States into the same godless pit Europe slid into decades ago. American Christians who travel to Europe are frequently stunned at how spiritually dark it is there, and at how little influence biblical ideas (or Bible-centered people) wield. They marvel that the very wellspring that produced

Aquinas, Luther, Calvin, Knox, Tyndale, Wycliffe, and the Wesley brothers could have now grown so desperately dry.

America's best hope for avoiding a similar future lies within those who are faithful to the biblical standards handed down to them from past generations. A vital, informed church, passionately living out the truth of the gospel, is just what the doctor ordered for America. In fact, the church of Jesus Christ *is* the doctor. But at this crucial moment in history, the physician is ailing.

Allow me to diagnose the symptoms. They manifest in four major areas.

1. Assimilation Syndrome—A people of maximum influence and cultural impact would follow Scripture's command to "not be conformed to this world, but be transformed by the renewing of your mind, that you may prove what is that good and acceptable and perfect will of God" (Romans 12:2). They would take to heart Jesus' declaration that we are the light and salt of the world, as well as His warning that salt which has lost its distinctive savor is worthless because it has lost its ability to act as a preservative (Matthew 5:13). And they would boldly live out the Master's desire that they be *in* the world, and yet not *of* it (John 17).

So how does our current generation of American believers measure up to that standard? It's not pretty. A wealth of research conducted over the last five or ten years—much of it by Christian pollster George Barna of Barna Research—tells an alarming story.

On the opening pages of his important book *The Second Coming of the Church*, Barna issues this stinging, but spot-on indictment of the American believer:

> Interestingly, the stumbling block for the Church is not its theology but its failure to apply what it believes in compelling ways. The downfall of the Church has not been the content of its message but its failure to practice those truths. Christians have been their own worst enemies when it comes to showing the world what authentic, biblical

Christianity looks like—and why it represents a viable alternative to materialism, existentialism, mysticism, and the other doctrines of popular culture.[24]

In category after category, born-again, Jesus-professing people show precious little difference in behaviors or demonstrated values than the unchurched and unsaved. For example:

- Today born-again married couples are no more likely to stay together than non-Christian couples. The divorce rates are virtually identical.[25]

  My wife Joni and I dated for seven years—our pastor and mentor, Dr. Lester Sumrall, referred to it, humorously, as the tribulation period—and we recently celebrated our twentieth wedding anniversary. It was a time of rejoicing for my family, but I was surprised at how excited people in our church became as we approached that milestone. I came to realize that one of the reasons our church was so thrilled is because so few preachers ever reach that point in their marriages.
- Born-again individuals were only slightly less likely to be on anti-depressant drugs (7 percent versus 8 percent).[26]
- One in five women having abortions were born-again or evangelical church-goers.[27]
- Born-again believers were only somewhat less likely to have purchased a lottery ticket recently (23 percent versus 27 percent).[28]
- In an average month, fewer than 10 percent of churched families prayed together other than at mealtimes.[29]
- Churched Christians gave away, on average, only three percent of their income in a typical year[30] and were less likely than unbelievers to have donated to a charity in the previous month.[31]
- The typical believer spent far less time reading the Bible than watching television.[32]

- If existing trends continue, the typical churched believer will live, grow fat, and die without leading a single person to Christ. In fact, at any given time, a majority of believers do not have even one specific unsaved person for whom they are praying.[33]
- Only 8 percent of senior pastors claim to have the gift of evangelism[34] and only 1 in 20 Christians make sharing their faith a part of their lifestyle.[35]

I could go on, but I don't want to send you into deep depression this early in the book. (Yes, there's more bad news coming, but hold on. Hope and solutions are coming too!)

All of this points to the fact that, in America, those who claim to have the distinction of having faith in God have been almost completely assimilated into the broader culture. The late pastor John Osteen put it this way: "The world has become so churchy and the church so worldly it is hard to tell the difference." And though that culture retains some faint remnants of the potent Puritan faith of the first American settlers, it also reflects large strains of nonbiblical and antibiblical thought.

2. Me-and-My-Comfort Syndrome—Biblically and historically, the decision to follow Christ was a decision that required "cost counting." It was a decision for sacrifice and service. Jesus said, "If any man will come after me, let him deny himself, and take up his cross, and follow me. For whosoever will save his life shall lose it: and whosoever will lose his life for my sake shall find it" (Matthew 16:24–25 KJV).

In other words, as I stated earlier, self-denial is "entry-level" Christianity.

Yet we live in a generation of believers that has seemingly made the cross a gateway for self-help and converted the call to a life of Christian service into a quest for comfort and pleasure. We want safety without sacrifice, victory without conflict, and wind and rain without thunder and lightning. We have become self-indulgent, self-seeking, and self-satisfied.

This is due, in no small measure, to a general decline of biblical preaching that began to take hold in the 1970s and accelerated throughout the 1980s. Pop psychology, rooted in humanist assumptions, began to supplant biblical principles in many pulpits. In some quarters, strong preaching—preaching that challenged saints to a life of sacrifice and equipped them for the rigors of service—deteriorated into little more than self-help homilies and success motivation rallies.

Our preachers are no longer prophets from out of the wilderness, clothed with camel hair and eating wild honey; they are slick-haired, shiny-shoed pulpiteers, selected by backslidden church boards not because of the life of God within them, but because of their carefully cultivated Las Vegas-style ability to dazzle this personality cult we used to call the church.

The pastoral imperative stopped being "Feed My sheep" and became "Entertain My sheep!" We have traded gospel preaching motivated by a heavenly desire for redemptive change for worldly diversions motivated by a sensual desire for temporal pleasure. We have Bozo the clown and Fufu the dog, we bring in Nashville retreads and Motown wannabes, we have fog machines, colored lights, TV cameras, and lots of action, we have padded pews and crystal chandeliers, but we manifest none of the power necessary to produce permanent change in the hearts of people.

As a result, we now have vast segments of the church that are self-oriented instead of others-oriented. They are inward-looking and comfort-seeking. They are therefore ill-equipped to challenge the dominant secular culture or lead through servanthood.

The order of the day is comfort, not conviction; rebellion, not repentance; family nights, not family altars. Religious institutions have become social clubs, better known for their adultery, alcoholism, and laziness than for their love for lost souls staggering toward the edge of eternity with no remedy in sight.

Our architecture is attractive, but our attitudes are repulsive. Our buildings are strong, but our character is weak. Our programs are well planned, but our relationships are neglected. We ritualize our religion, but reject any resemblance of the victory and vitality of a life fully surrendered to Christ. It is little wonder we have lost our appeal.

The secular world, with hunger in its eyes and a hole in its heart, looks to the church, and to its chagrin, finds no love, no life, no laughter; no hope, no help, and no happiness. Gazing at the church whose garments are tainted, tattered, and torn, the world woefully exclaims, "Why would I want to be a part of that? They're obviously more miserable than me."

3. Withdrawal and Isolation Syndrome—Today, it is customary to judge the effectiveness or success of a ministry by how many people come to its worship services. In ages past, the standard of success was not how many people were coming, but how many people were going—going into the culture of which they were a part to live a transformed life, especially in the presence of ridicule and persecution.

The failure of the church to actively, vigorously, and positively engage the culture has led to defeatism and isolation. The current generation of believers has failed to meet the culture squarely in the marketplace of ideas and present a relevant, compelling gospel. The implications of that failure are troubling. We have forfeited leadership in each of the seven spheres of society: home; the church; education; media; the arts (including entertainment and sports); commerce, science, and technology; and government and politics.

Some have described this trend as the "privatizing" of the Christian faith. For most of the church's two-thousand-year history, Christians understood that faith and biblical principles infused every aspect of life and existence. No one compartmentalized his life in such a way as to create a "private" sphere for his faith and a Christless "public" sphere for his work. His educational, social, political and cultural life and hobbies were not separated from his devotion to God. Jesus *was* all, and was *in* all.

But today many Christians have just such a compartmentalized view of their lives. Nancy Pearcey, in her excellent book *Total Truth: Liberating Christianity from Its Cultural Captivity*, observes:

Polls consistently show that a large percentage of Americans claim to believe in God or to be born again—yet the effect of Christian principles is decreasing in public life. Why? Because most evangelicals have little training in how to frame Christian worldview principles in a language applicable in the public square. Though Christianity is thriving in modern culture, it is at the expense of being ever more firmly relegated to the private sphere.[36]

Far too many of God's people have bought in to the secularists' big lie—namely, that matters of faith are purely a personal and private matter. Once a believer accepts that premise, he has surrendered all ability to follow Jesus' command to "let your light so shine before men, that they may see your good works and glorify your Father in heaven" (Matthew 5:16).

Believers have been intimidated into silence because of their perception of being in the minority. They have succumbed to what one researcher dubbed the "spiral of silence,"[37] a term that refers to people's willingness to speak up when they believe they are in the majority, and their reluctance to do so when they perceive their point of view is not the prevalent one.

The truth is more valuable than anyone's opinion, regardless of how well read, well bred or well fed they may appear to be. We, as believers, must never again allow some bearded old goat sitting in a university chair to stare at us over the brim of his glasses, stroke his whiskers, suck on a pipe and crown his head with an encircling wreath of smoke and intimidate us because he feels he has some kind of intellectual superiority over us. The believer must stand in possession of absolute truth and never relinquish his ground. We must remember that truth always prevails. It may be banned, blocked, burned, or buried in a borrowed tomb, but it cannot be stopped. It will resurrect itself and beat the pall bearers back to the house. Jesus said in John 14:6, "I am the way, the *TRUTH*, and the life." Don't allow anyone to ever intimidate you into backing down from the truth.

As one astute observer wrote recently:

But while Christians are at the forefront of the cultural debate, they are not generally at the forefront of the battles to recapture a Christian culture. They do not think of a distinctly Christian mission in art, music, education, business, technology, politics, the economy and other areas of culture. Christians, in fact, are not winning today's culture wars, *because they have never fought them*. They are not fighting them because they no longer have any aptitude for cultural leadership. They have no aptitude for cultural leadership because they have no interest in it. They have no interest in cultural leadership because they do not see culture as a religious calling. For the vast majority of Christians, culture is simply beyond the sphere of their concern.[38]

In other words, we've wanted nothing more from the culture than to be left alone. "Let us have our Christian television network, a few radio stations, and our own bookstores, and we'll leave you alone too." The problem with that is, we're not called and commissioned to leave them alone. Jesus said He was sending the power of His Holy Spirit to equip and energize an army of "witnesses."

This tendency toward withdrawal and isolation is the third reason the doctor (the church in America) is too sick to bring the healing our ailing culture so desperately needs.

4. Worldview Confusion Syndrome—Here's one more Barna statistic for you: Only 9 percent of all born-again adults have a biblical worldview.[39]

Of course, *worldview* is a buzzword that is thrown around freely these days. And I've used it repeatedly on the preceding pages without defining what I mean by it. Just what is a worldview? What does a biblical worldview look like? And why does it matter so much? I'll show you in the coming pages. And as we'll discover, understanding the power and origins of currently competing worldviews is the very key to winning the battle we face today.

ACTION POINTS

- Resist assimilation. Fight to follow Jesus' command to be "in the world, but not of it."
- De-compartmentalize your faith. Identify any areas of your life not fully informed by and infused with biblical truth. Then take steps to learn and apply biblical assumptions in those areas.
- Don't make an idol of comfort. Embrace the rigors of discipleship and the joys of selfless sacrifice.
- Reject the secularists' "big lie"—namely, that matters of faith are purely a personal and private matter.
- Suggested reading:

  A Jealous God: Science's Crusade Against Religion, by Pamela R. Winnick[40]

  Total Truth: Liberating Christianity from Its Cultural Captivity, by Nancy Pearcey[41]

  Silent No More: Bringing Moral Clarity to America While Freedom Still Rings, by Rod Parsley[42]

  Persecution: How Liberals are Waging War Against Christianity, by David Limbaugh[43]

two

WHY WORLDVIEWS MATTER

On Tuesday morning, April 20, 1999, Eric Harris and Dylan Klebold strolled into their Colorado high school wearing trench coats and lugging duffel bags stuffed with sawed-off shotguns, rifles, semi-automatic pistols, and pipe bombs. What they did over the next fifty-five minutes is widely known.

What is less well known is that the first victim of that tragedy, Rachel Scott, was a genuine Christian who was neither ashamed nor afraid to affirm her faith. Some time after the shootings occurred, I had the opportunity to talk to a well dressed businessman with hollow eyes. It was Rachel's father. We were standing near the school as we spoke.

"On Rachel's birthday those two walked right past where we're standing now," he told me. "They walked right over there where Rachel was sitting beside that little tree. She was eating her lunch, talking with one of her friends. They walked up to her, Pastor Parsley, and they asked her, 'Do you believe in God?'"

"With a slight grin, she responded, 'Well, yes, why?'"

"And one of them pulled a 12 gauge shotgun from underneath his trench coat . . . and my daughter became their first victim."

The tragedy at Columbine High School stands as the deadliest school shooting spree in U.S. history.

What is not as widely recognized is the specific bundle of ideas, beliefs, and assumptions that made such a murder spree *thinkable*— much less *doable*. That bundle could be called Harris and Klebold's shared "worldview." It was the distorted lens through which they viewed themselves, their world, and the other people in it.

The *American Heritage Dictionary* defines the term *worldview* as "(1) The overall perspective from which one sees and interprets the world; or (2) A collection of beliefs about life and the universe held by an individual or a group."

Let's consider the "beliefs about life and the universe" these two young men picked up during their brief lives. Put another way, let's ask, "How do you construct the worldview of someone who could do such things?"

First, you must relentlessly teach him that everything in the physical universe (including himself) is the product of random chance. All order . . . all beauty . . . all life is purely accidental. There is no designer who can give his life meaning or who might hold him accountable for his actions. Make sure he understands that because all life, including human life, is accidental, there is no ultimate authority who sets standards of "right" and "wrong." In fact, consistently reinforce that there is no such thing as absolute right and wrong—that old, repressive concepts such as morality and sin are outdated and have been scientifically "proven" to be artificial creations designed to keep people in line. (Therefore, you must keep him out of Bible-teaching churches at all costs.)

Declare that "truth" is whatever is "true" for you. Another person's truth might be different from your own.

Be sure to emphasize that humans are just another species of animal —uniquely evolved animals, to be sure—but animals just the same. Declare that human life is not intrinsically more precious than that of a tree frog in the Amazon. Frequently use the language of "rights" in regard to animals. Encourage deep concern for the way chickens are housed on egg farms, but condemn those who have qualms about partial birth abortions.

Even better, frequently characterize humans as a kind of viral blight on the planet—a scourge bringing nothing but environmental catastrophe and "habitat destruction" wherever they spread.

Next, allow him to fill his soul with death metal music. Let him marinate in chaotic, angry songs that glorify mayhem, ugliness, violence, and death.

For the finishing touch, cultivate an obsession with "first-person-shooter" computer games—the more graphic the better. Make sure that by the time he reaches the tender age of sixteen, he's already killed thousands of people or creatures "virtually" with realistic splatter and gore. As you do, keep in mind that studies in neuroscience have shown that the human brain treats vividly imagined events and real ones almost identically.

Thus, when the time comes to level a real shotgun at a real schoolmate, any tendency toward remorse or conscience will have been eliminated. He will have already been "there" many times before.

To summarize, if you're going to create the young man who will point a pistol at the head of a young Christian girl like Rachel Scott, or her more popularized schoolmate, Cassie Bernall,[1] and ask, "Do you believe in God?" then, when she answers "Yes," will pull the trigger—you're going to have to eliminate God, truth, judgment, eternity, and any lingering sense that human life has sacred value.

In other words, you must construct a specific worldview. And that is precisely what happened with Klebold and Harris. (That worldview could be labeled nihilism, which we will examine a little farther on. By the way, it's growing in popularity!)

I have used this most extreme of examples to illustrate a vital point: Worldviews matter.

No, not every person who holds atheist and evolutionary beliefs is a killer in the making. And yes, the overwhelming majority of people who love death metal music or play Doom III and Quake IV would never hurt a fellow human being. But that doesn't diminish the force of this truth—a person's worldview directly determines his or her attitudes and actions, values and choices.

In other words, worldview is destiny—for individuals and for civilizations. Let me show you why.

"ISMS" AND SCHISMS

More and more Christian leaders and thinkers now recognize that worldview is *the* hinge on which our battle for America will turn. In the introduction to his book *Heretics*, G. K. Chesterton saw the importance of worldview back in 1905 and wrote:

> There are some people, nevertheless—and I am one of them—who think that the most practical and important thing about a man is still his view of the universe. We think that for a landlady considering a lodger, it is important to know his income, but still more important to know his philosophy. We think that for a general about to fight an enemy, it is important to know the enemy's numbers, but still more important to know the enemy's philosophy. **We think the question is not whether the theory of the cosmos affects matters, but whether, in the long run, anything else affects them.**[2] (emphasis added)

More recently, Charles Colson has written of his belief in the power of worldview to impact society:

> This is the challenge for the church today. There has never been a time when the transformation brought about by Christian faith has been so greatly needed . . . Unfortunately, too many Christians have disregarded Christ's command to occupy and transform the culture, and the absence of a Christian voice in the public square has only compounded our problems. **Before we can make a real and lasting difference in the culture, we must understand how the biblical worldview connects us with every aspect of the creation.**[3] (emphasis added)

I agree! I see this more clearly now than ever before. A key to restoration and wholeness for our culture lies in people of faith forming, proclaiming, and contending publicly for a biblical worldview. But at this pivotal moment in history, far too many Christians have unknowingly absorbed elements of false and unbiblical belief systems.

Up to this point you've already seen me refer to a number of different "isms." I've referenced humanism, atheism, and nihilism. I could also mention Marxism/communism, socialism, and New Age mysticism (and believe me, I will before I'm finished!). These are all worldviews to some degree. And all of these are fairly familiar to most Christians. Most of us have at least a general understanding of the "gist" of these belief systems and are aware that they conflict with Christian belief in certain ways.

What many of my fellow believers *don't* have is a grasp of why people cling to these competing worldviews so tightly when they so clearly don't work very well and run counter to evidence and experience.

For example, Marxism/communism is a colossal failure in every respect. Not one of Karl Marx's confident predictions about the course of history has been borne out. His economic theories are utterly discredited. And history has clearly shown that wherever Marxism became the dominant paradigm, individual liberty perished, living standards plummeted, and multitudes died. Nevertheless, you'll find ardent believers in Marxism all over America and Europe. Our university faculties are filled with Marx admirers.

How can this be?

The answer lies in the power of presuppositions. Let me show you what I mean.

THE HIDDEN FOUNDATION OF EVERY WORLDVIEW

Years ago, a good classical education would have included at least one course in logic. One of the first things you would have learned in such a class is that all "propositions" (assertions of truth) rest on certain assumptions or "givens." In other words, logical conclusions are built upon a set of assumptions. These assumptions are sometimes called presuppositions because they involve *pre*supposing that certain things are true.

Before the fifteenth century, many navigators feared that you would fall off the edge of the earth if you sailed too far west. Why? Because their underlying assumption was that the earth was flat and therefore had an edge. Their logic was quite sound. But their conclusion was wrong because it was built upon a false presupposition.

If your logic is sound, you will reach a correct conclusion, but only *if* your assumptions are correct. But if one or more of your starting assumptions are false, you can have airtight, foolproof reasoning and logic—but come up with a very wrong conclusion. Allow me to illustrate what I'm talking about.

In the fourteenth century, a plague known as the Black Death was ravaging Europe. At one point, it was widely believed that the plague was being spread by cats, because there always seemed to be a large number of cats present wherever the deadly disease emerged. So, in many cities, cats were killed by the thousands in the hopes of stopping the spread of the contagion. It was all very logical and reasonable.

Of course, we now know that the Black Death was carried by a type of flea, which tended to infest rats. By killing most of their local cats, many cities actually made the problem much, much worse. Before the plague had run its course in Europe, more than twenty-four million people had died.

Logical, rational conclusions based upon faulty premises are still killing people today. And as with the plague, false presuppositions frequently result in solutions that end up making worse the ill they are attempting to cure!

You see, presuppositions don't just underlie theories about navigation and disease. They are also at the root of every worldview. Here's another example.

Around the year 1800, mathematician Thomas Malthus did some calculations on population growth and determined that in a very few decades earth's population would have grown so large that food and resources would be exhausted—resulting in mass starvation and suffering.

Malthus was a brilliant mathematician. There were no errors in his calculations. And yet every prediction he made failed to materialize. In fact, just the opposite proved to be true. Why? Because he built his model on two assumptions: That populations would always increase at the same rate, never leveling off or declining. And that the ability to produce food through farming would stay roughly the same. Both assumptions proved to be completely wrong.[4]

It is now universally understood that as societies develop and living standards increase, populations tend to level off and even decline. Today most countries in the Northern Hemisphere actually have a negative birthrate—meaning that not enough babies are being born to replace the older folks who are dying off. As a matter of fact, a few years ago population researchers predicted that the earth's population would level off in the year 2050, but now some analysts think the world may already be hitting that point![5]

At the same time, constant advances in farming methods have made it possible to produce ever more food on less and less land. The fact is, most hunger that exists in the world today is the result of war, bad government, and/or bad religion—not overpopulation. (Of course, that doesn't mean we, as Christians, have any less responsibility to try to ease their suffering if we can.)

With Malthus we once again have airtight logic producing a false conclusion. Why? It is because Malthus built the elegant house of his argument on a shifting-sand foundation of faulty presuppositions. The same is true for most people who hold nonbiblical worldviews today.

Like Karl Marx, Malthus gave birth to a whole movement. People who have embraced his gospel of scarcity are called "Malthusians." And as was the case for Marx, even though Malthusian predictions have failed to manifest again and again, you find his disciples everywhere, particularly on college faculties. His assertion that overpopulation is a serious problem is an absolute article of faith among environmentalists today. *Faith* is the right word because they hold fast to this belief in the face of overwhelming evidence to the contrary.

That it is a bad thing when human beings reproduce themselves has become a "given" in their worldview. It is presuppositional.

All of this means that the true root of the current cultural divide is that we are operating from differing sets of assumptions. It's not that whole segments of society are irrational or unintelligent. They have very rationally come to some erroneous conclusions because they have bought in to a specific set of false assumptions. The biblical term for this is *deception*. They have been deceived, as Paul warned Timothy in 2 Timothy 3:13: "But evil men and imposters will grow worse and worse, deceiving and being deceived."

Nevertheless, for all people, the powerful temptation is to view those who disagree with us as stupid, crazy, or evil. Browse the comments section of any issue-oriented Internet site and you'll see what I mean. The language of "stupid, crazy, and evil" fills the message boards.

Take a random glance at any of the discussion forums of the popular left-liberal Web site The Democratic Underground (www.democraticunderground.com), and you'll see what I mean. But be warned, you'll be exposed to torrents of profanity and vulgarity that would enrich a rapper's vocabulary.

For example, here's a sampling of the (printable) comments left on a discussion thread with the heading "Slamming Ann Coulter."[6] Watch carefully for the language of "stupid, crazy, or evil." Any spelling and grammatical errors were in the original comments:

> Any intelligent right-winger . . . Oh wait . . . That's an oxymoron. Sorry about that. But I was going to say that any intelligent right-winger would shed her, her poor logic and nonsensical critical thinking skills, and her hatred of everyone for next year's election, but I guess hatred is a prominent plank in their platform.

She brings new meaning to the phrase "dumb blond". In fact, she is so—whatever—I would not even put her in that class because it's an insult to real dumb blonds that are not evil people.

Queen of the Damned . . . . . While we laugh and make fun of Anne Coulter . . . . the right wing wacko's take her seriously, as she parrots what they really think. This is some scary stuff. It concerns me that anyone would take her seriously, but she's if you think about it, she represents the best advertising AGAINST Bush.

I am sure there are millions of ditto heads that feed off her sociopathic rants—She is a dangerous nut case

This is a sicko boob who happens to get TV exposure by Right Wingnuts for her HYPERACTIVE ORANGUTANG? APPEARANCE. Paint her face Orange!

To be fair, many passionate people on the Right participate in very much the same thing—including some of the Christian Right. Some Christians go so far as to maintain that advocates of liberal policies can't just be sincerely and logically wrong because they are deceived; they must be evil and seen to be operating from the darkest possible motives. There are times when the Left gets it right and the Right gets it wrong, and there are other times that someone like Samuel, the prophet of ancient Israel, needs to stand up between two extremes and declare, "You're both wrong!"

Yet, in this current climate, opponents are never simply mistaken—they "lie." They never sincerely disagree; they are "sick," "twisted," "demented," or "feebleminded." Yet as we have seen, two highly intelligent, rational, and good-hearted people can come to view the world very differently, simply because they are starting from differing sets of assumptions about what is true.

Christian academic and author James Sire clearly had the power of presuppositions to shape worldviews in mind when he drafted this excellent definition:

> A worldview is a commitment, a fundamental orientation of the heart, that can be expressed as a story or a set of presuppositions (assumptions which may be true, partially true or entirely false) which we hold (consciously or subconsciously; consistently or inconsistently) about the basic constitution of reality and that provides the foundation on which we live and move and have our being.[7]

Dr. Sire correctly points out that a worldview is a "set of presuppositions" and that those assumptions which undergird a worldview can be "true, partially true or entirely false." The problem is that, by their very nature, presuppositions tend to go unquestioned and unexamined. Once you accept something as a "given"—once you begin to *assume* a certain thing is true—you stop wondering about its validity.

So, if we are going to understand the various worldviews that are now competing for the hearts and minds of our fellow citizens, we're going to have to do more than just explore their basic tenets. We must expose the unexamined assumptions upon which those worldviews are built.

THE ANATOMY OF A WORLDVIEW

By now, I'm sure you have begun to appreciate how important this issue of worldview is to the current struggle within our nation. As one college textbook on worldviews states:

> Because worldviews are pertinent to every person's life—the way we think and the way we act—and because virtually all worldviews promise salvation or utopia, the study of worldviews is of critical importance.[8]

But what are the components of a full-featured worldview? This is a question we must answer before we can give any of the competing worldviews a valid examination or establish the components of a thoroughly biblical one.

In his excellent book *The Universe Next Door,* James Sire lays out seven basic questions every major worldview tries to answer:[9]

1. What is prime reality—the really real?
2. What is the nature of external reality, that is, the world around us?
3. What is a human being?
4. What happens to a person at death?
5. Why is it possible to know anything at all?
6. How do we know what is right and wrong?
7. What is the meaning of human history?

Of course, as we'll see in the next chapter, biblical Christianity provides clear, consistent answers to each of these questions. But other worldviews claim to offer answers to these questions as well.

In the coming pages, I'll use these questions as a framework for briefly examining some of the prominent worldviews today and for exposing the false assumptions on which they're built. Stay with me here because the terms we define now will become important.

Do worldviews matter? More than you can imagine. Let me show you why.

ACTION POINTS

- Reject the language of "Stupid, Crazy or Evil" when characterizing people who disagree with you.
- Practice identifying the false assumptions underlying the arguments of those who hold anti-biblical worldviews and learn to challenge those assumptions with respect and grace.
- Visit Focus on the Family's "The Truth Project" at www.TheTruthProject.org and find out how to receive training as a "change agent" who is a skilled advocate for a biblical worldview.
- Visit www.ChristianWorldview.net and explore ways the biblical truth speaks to realms such as Music, Economics, Bio-Ethics and the Environment.
- Suggested reading:

A Christian Manifesto, by Francis Schaeffer[10]
Naming the Elephant: Worldview as a Concept, by James W. Sire[11]

three

PRETENDERS TO THE THRONE

Worldviews are like pituitary glands. Every living person has one—whether he knows it or not. In *Future Shock,* Alvin Toffler described them as the "mental model of the world" each of us carries in his head.[1]

When singer-songwriter Sheryl Crow, referring to the expected U.S. invasion of Iraq, says, "I think war is based in greed and there are huge karmic retributions that will follow. I think war is never the answer to solving any problems. The best way to solve problems is to not have enemies,"[2] she's giving us some insight into her worldview.

When the late science writer Carl Sagan declared, "The Cosmos is all there is or ever was or ever will be,"[3] he made clear the cornerstone of his worldview too.

And when Peter Singer, current holder of the prestigious Ira DeCamp Professorship in Bioethics at Princeton University, writes, "Human babies are not born self-aware, or capable of grasping that they exist over time. They are not persons," and writes that "animals are self-aware," and therefore, "the life of a newborn is of less value than the life of a pig, a dog, or a chimpanzee,"[4] he is revealing quite a bit about his worldview as well.

Worldviews, however, are not the exclusive domain of celebrities, scientists, and Ivy League professors. As I stated above, everyone has a worldview. An illiterate peasant on the plains of Mongolia has a grid for understanding and interpreting his world. So does the jobless Palestinian protester burning a Danish flag and shouting "Death to Denmark." And so do you and I.

The real question is, are our worldviews based upon accurate assumptions or false ones? As we saw in the previous chapter, you can reach some very logical conclusions that are absolutely worthless if you start from a single faulty presupposition. We also saw that all worldviews tend to be constructed out of answers to some basic questions. Questions such as:

Where did the world come from?
What is a human being?
What happens when we die?
How do we know what is right and wrong? (Or is there any
   such thing?)

Answer those questions a certain way, and you'll find yourself agreeing with Peter Singer that babies with severe disabilities should be killed (and then trying to decide whose definition of *severe* should be used).

As I stated at the outset, worldview is destiny, for individuals and for civilizations. But at the most basic level, at the core of every worldview, is an answer (right or wrong) to one key question: Who (or what) is God? Or, put another way, who is mankind's Messiah?

Before exploring a biblical worldview, let's explore how some of today's dominant and rising worldviews answer that question. Who are the pretenders to the throne of God?

HUMANISM: MAN = GOD

Sometimes the terms *humanism* and *secular humanism* are used without distinction, but the fact is, there are several flavors of this widespread worldview.

By their own definition, humanists are those who believe in the primacy of the human being. There are, oddly enough, religious humanists who believe in a God or gods, and some form of universal moral order. These people embrace the term *humanist* in the sense that they care deeply about the well-being of other human beings. But this group is clearly the runt of the humanist litter. In fact, the term *secular humanist* was created with purpose by the dominant branch of the family tree that wanted to distinguish itself by its atheism.

The basic tenets of humanism have been outlined in three "manifestos."

The original Humanist Manifesto was written in 1933 by Unitarian minister Raymond Bragg and initially cosigned by thirty-four other intellectuals, academics, and Unitarian clerics. In the years that followed, many other "progressive" thinkers added their names to the declaration. But unlike the Humanist Manifestos that would come later (H.M. II in 1973; and H.M. III in 2003), this document was honest enough to state the obvious—that humanism is an attempt at creating a new-and-improved religion. In the opening paragraphs of the document we find:

Today man's larger understanding of the universe, his scientific achievements, and deeper appreciation of brotherhood, have created a situation which requires a new statement of the means and purposes of religion. Such a vital, fearless, and frank religion capable of furnishing adequate social goals and personal satisfactions may appear to many people as a complete break with the past. While this age does owe a vast debt to the traditional religions, it is nonetheless obvious that any religion that can hope to be a synthesizing and dynamic force for today must be shaped for the needs of this age. **To establish such a religion is a major necessity of the present.** (emphasis added)[5]

Humanists, although overwhelmingly atheist or agnostic, are not a people without a messiah. Their savior is humanity itself. As Humanist

Manifesto II declares: "[H]umans are responsible for what we are or will become. No deity will save us; we must save ourselves."[6] That lays it out there pretty clearly, doesn't it? "We have met the messiah, and he is us."

Of course, humanist ideas weren't a twentieth-century invention. They go back a little farther—as far as the Garden of Eden. Professor Herbert Schlossberg has written, "Eve was the first humanist."[7] He was referring to the appeal the serpent made to Eve's pride when he said, "You will not surely die. For God knows that in the day you eat of it your eyes will be opened, and you will be like God, knowing good and evil" (Genesis 3:4–5).

"You will be like God." That's the seductive line for which people have been falling for millennia.

Of this deception, Schlossberg also wrote:

The serpent tempted her with a religious argument. She could be like God, having knowledge and power. She could be wise apart from God . . . The physical attraction of the fruit was intended to be [secondary]. What was to be fed was her pride, and what would grow was her appetite for self-worship.[8]

That appetite is certainly in evidence when you read humanist literature. The original Humanist Manifesto outlined fifteen affirmations of this new "vital, fearless, and frank religion." Many of these points speak directly to the seven questions James Sire said every worldview claims to answer.

Sire's first two worldview questions are essentially *What is really real? and* What is the nature of the world around us?

To this, the first of the statements in Humanist Manifesto I replies: "Religious humanists regard the universe as self-existing and not created." In a similar vein, the primary author of Humanist Manifesto II, Paul Kurtz, has said, "Humanism cannot in any fair sense of the word apply to one who still believes in God as the source and creator of the universe."[9] In other words, you can't be a bona fide, capital "*H*"

Humanist if you believe in God. To the true Humanist, God didn't create man. Man created God.

Now as we've seen, assumptions have implications—and the assumption that there is no Creator-God carries some huge ones! As I pointed out in the extreme case of Klebold and Harris, if there is no Creator, then there is no higher meaning to existence. And no ultimate judge of our actions.

The next two questions on Sire's list—What is a human being? and What happens to a person at death?—are also directly addressed in the Humanist Manifesto.

The second assertion of the Manifesto states: "Humanism believes that man is a part of nature and that he has emerged as a result of a continuous process." In other words, science is the only proper tool for understanding who we are, just as it is the vehicle for understanding any other "part of nature."

As to the question whether or not the flame of our conscious existence will continue to burn after death, the humanist answer is, "Don't get your hopes up, friend":

> We assume that humanism will take the path of social and mental hygiene and discourage sentimental and unreal hopes and wishful thinking. (11th assertion)
>
> Religious Humanism considers the complete realization of human personality to be the end of man's life and seeks its development and fulfillment in the here and now. (12th assertion)

Did you catch that? Hoping for an afterlife is bad "mental hygiene." It's unclean. Of course, this humanist assumption of no-life-after-death carries major implications for thought and action. In fact, it is a prescription for selfishness overlaid with hopelessness. And in thirty years of pastoring I have seen up close how devastating to the human soul and body that dark combination can be.

This is just the briefest of introductions to humanism. We'll explore this false but seductive philosophy in much greater depth and trace its destructive heritage in upcoming chapters. But for now, I just want to define terms and acquaint you with the basic distinctives of each system of belief.

MARXISM/STATISM: GOVERNMENT = GOD

Humanism shares a common intellectual ancestry and many common assumptions with the worldview that bears the name of Karl Marx (1818–83).

Marx was an atheist long before he was a socialist or the ideological father of modern communism. In fact, his rejection of God was the starting point and foundation of everything else he came to espouse. This militant atheism is one of several attributes Marxism shares with its cousin, secular humanism.

Marx's atheism was inspired by the contemporary German philosopher Ludwig Feuerbach. As one scholar described it, "Marx accepted Feuerbach's thesis that the only god of man is man himself."[10] I have to be honest with you, if you and I are the only god we have, we're both in deep trouble! My personal experience and history agree—when we try to fix things on our own, we make an unholy mess of it every time.

As you probably know, the movement to which Marx gave his name is a radical form of socialism that rejects the notions of private property, free enterprise, and personal responsibility upon which capitalism is built. I can't help but be amused at politicians and entertainers who spout socialist rhetoric while enjoying the benefits socialism could never provide. If they really believed what they were saying, why wouldn't they give up their cribs and their cars, and live out the conclusions of those they say they admire?

Marx saw himself as a champion of the poor, exploited working classes. With the conviction of a prophet, he believed natural and economic forces were moving history toward a predetermined end— a series of upheavals, or revolutions, that would result in "the dictatorship of the proletariat."

In other words, he foresaw a utopia, or paradise on earth, in which there would be no extremes of poverty or wealth, no rich ruling class, and each person's labor would be filled with purpose and dignity as it served the greater "collective" good of society.

To Europe's millions of hardworking poor in the early stages of the industrial revolution—particularly in places like czarist Russia—that all looked pretty attractive on paper. But of course, Marxism hasn't worked out quite so well for common folks in actual practice!

It is conservatively estimated that in a mere handful of decades, more than twenty million people in the former Soviet Union died in Lenin's and Stalin's political purges, government-induced famines, and the infamous gulags. In China, as Mao took Marx's theology and used it as a road map for a "Cultural Revolution" and "The Great Leap Forward"—upwards of sixty million people either starved or were killed. In Vietnam, more than 850,000 died in "reeducation camps" after the withdrawal of the American military presence.[11]

Recent research has estimated the twentieth century's "victims of communism" at more than one hundred million in number.[12]

I have had the opportunity to see firsthand the effects of Communism. I was staying in one of Leningrad's finer hotels, and those in my group ordered beef for dinner.

"We're sorry," our waiter replied, "you had beef last night."

"That's right," we said. "We would like beef again tonight, please."

"You don't understand," came the reply. "Last night when six of you ordered beef, it was our hotel's total allotment of beef for one month. Tonight we have chicken."

So we ate chicken that night, and were glad to get it!

I was privileged to see the red flag of the USSR come down and the red, white, and blue banner of the Russian Republic raised during the civil unrest that led to the ouster of Mikhail Gorbachev and the eventual breakup of the Soviet empire. I saw firsthand the statue of Lenin fall under the sledgehammers of those who felt the first reverberations of freedom among a generation that had known nothing but totalitarianism. I remember standing in the great Lenin Sports Arena in the city of St. Petersburg (formerly Leningrad) in the first gospel crusade in Russia in over seventy years. I watched with awe as row after row of soldiers of the Red Army came from the upper levels of that stadium and came to the altar in response to the message of the cross, which they were hearing for the very first time. What a contrast to the physical deprivation, emotional uncertainty and spiritual devastation that was all they had known during the reign of Communism!

However, suffering and death on this massive scale aren't just a relic of the last century. As I write, millions are starving and dying in North Korea—one of the few remaining unapologetically Communist nations on earth. Although good information is always hard to come by in a Marxist dictatorship, one study estimated that in a recent five-year period, between two and three million North Koreans had died of starvation. [13]

All this misery and heartache was made possible, in fact *inevitable*, by the underlying assumptions of the Marxist worldview.

One of those key assumptions is that religious belief is a major obstacle to the creation of a "workers' paradise" and thus must be stamped out at all cost.

Also, because Marxism rejects the biblical view of man as fallen, sinful, and in need of redemption, it carries the opposite assumption—that man is basically good and perfectible. It is man's environment—the system in which he lives—that makes him selfish and brutish. Therefore, Marx and friends reasoned, absolute power to control man's environment had to be vested in the government. As long as any power, property, or freedom of choice remained with the individual, utopia could never be created.

That's why wherever Marxism has been planted in fertile soil, tyranny has bloomed.

Today, a modified form of this worldview is very much alive around the world and even here in the United States. It is one that shares many of the same assumptions, but pursues the logical conclusions that flow from those assumptions in a somewhat kinder, gentler way.

I'm referring to statism, the belief that government can and should provide a solution to every problem and meet every human need. It is enlightened-government-as-messiah. As with Marxism, the presupposition at the root of this conclusion is a rejection of the Bible's depiction of man as fallen and sinful—what theologians would call the doctrine of original sin.

If, contrary to what the Bible declares, people are born basically good, then there must be some other explanation for why people hoard wealth while others suffer lack, steal, cheat, rape, molest, and kill. If the problem isn't *internal* to man (a fallen nature), it must be *external*. We don't have paradise on earth because we haven't created the right environment. And we can't create the right environment unless we grant the government enough power and resources to build it.

Watch your national or local news on any given night and you'll see evidence of this logic in discussions about public policy and government programs. For example, when a new report comes out about a surge in AIDS or other sexually transmitted diseases, you will invariably hear an expert declare that we have to have more "education" to combat the problem. The assumption is that it is only a lack of information that causes people to act irresponsibly toward themselves and others.

Of course, there is probably not a person in America who is unaware that having unprotected, nonmonogamous sex, or sharing dirty needles, is an invitation to a legion of diseases. A lack of information is not the heart of the problem; a need for inner transformation is.

Name any current social ill and you'll find a chorus of voices crying for greater "investment" on the part of government, more "programs," increased "regulation," and, of course, better "education" to increase "awareness."

As prevalent as this worldview is here in America, it is even more dominant in the United Kingdom and continental Europe. Why? Because their abandonment of biblical concepts like the fall (man's rejection of God's authority, choosing instead to rebel and go his own way by yielding to the temptation of the devil) happened much earlier and to a much greater degree than in the United States. Keep in mind, Europe has declared itself fully "post-Christian." Thus in Great Britain today, there is a tendency to point a finger of blame at the government for every negative act of man or nature.

Here's a stunning example. In May of 2005, a single mother in England named Julie Atkins made headlines when, before national news cameras, she blamed the government for failing her and her daughters.

You see, all three of her daughters were about to be single mothers as well. What were these girls' ages at the time of their concurrent pregnancies? Fifteen, fourteen, and twelve. Here is this mom's statement to a national newspaper:

> "Frankly, I blame the schools," Ms. Atkins told *The Sun*. "More and more kids are getting pregnant younger and younger and sex education needs to start a lot earlier."[14]

She went on to cast ultimate blame on the British government. The example is outrageous, but the phenomenon is common.

Here at home, every headline-grabbing natural disaster and spectacular crime is immediately followed by a frenzy to assign "blame" to the appropriate government official or agency (witness the aftermath of Hurricane Katrina).

Of course, such blame is never laid upon the actual disaster or criminal—that would give credence to the idea that we live in a fallen world. And that is antithetical to the Marxist/statist worldview.

MATERIALISM/NATURALISM: THE COSMOS = GOD

Our world is morally upside down. We preserve nature but abort babies. We have developed the technology to build strong, solid houses, but have weak, sick homes. We are smarter but no wiser, and we know more but understand less. We go faster, but we get nowhere. We have conquered space, but our habits have conquered us. We rescue the whales and the whooping cranes, but neglect and abuse our own children. At the root of it all is materialism.

When the subject is worldviews, the terms *materialist* and *materialism* don't mean what they do when we use them in normal conversation. When Madonna sang "living in a material world and I am a material girl" back in the 1980s, she was proudly claiming to be *materialistic* in the commonly used sense—that is, being overly devoted to wealth and possessions.

When philosophers and theologians talk about materialism, however, they're referring to a belief system that claims the *material* universe is all there is. In other words, there is no unseen *spiritual* realm that lies beyond the physical world. Carl Sagan was making a confident profession of materialism when he said, as noted above: "The Cosmos is all there is or ever was or ever will be."

His statement seems to be a deliberate mirror of the Bible's triple declaration that God is He "who is and who was and who is to come" (Revelation 1:4; 1:8; 4:8). In mimicking the Bible's language about God, Sagan was pointing us to a key aspect of the materialist worldview. He was saying, "Don't look for God or anything else outside of a physical, measurable, scientifically comprehensible universe. Because that's all there is."

His statement attempts to deliver materialism's answer to those first two of Dr. Sire's seven questions: What is prime reality—the really real? And what is the nature of external reality, that is, the world around us?

This worldview also goes by the name naturalism because of its core belief that *nature* is all there is, and that there are no processes at work in the universe other than *natural* ones. In other words, there are no *supernatural* forces.

What is naturalism's view of man? Not surprisingly, it's pretty low. An old joke that has circulated for years about a group of people in ancient Israel that denied the influence and reality of the supernatural goes like this: "The Sadducees did not believe in heaven, in angels, or in the supernatural—that is why they were sad, you see."

You may be surprised to learn that you and I are just organized assemblages of atoms—as are beetles, rocks, stars, and toothbrushes. Former Supreme Court Justice Oliver Wendell Holmes Jr. said so explicitly when he wrote: "I see no reason for attributing to man a significance different in kind from that which belongs to a baboon or a grain of sand."[15] To the materialist, your consciousness, personality, creativity, and emotions are a happy accident of nature driven purely by chemical reactions and neuro-electrical impulses.

James Sire sums up the materialist view of man like this: "Human beings are complex 'machines'; personality is an interrelation of physical and chemical properties we do not yet fully understand."[16] And as we saw in Chapter 1, there is a growing movement among materialist researchers toward reducing all religious experience and spiritual hunger down to brain chemistry and genetic mutation, as Dean Hamer has done in his book, *The God Gene.*[17]

Given all of that, you probably can guess how the materialist/naturalist answers the question, What happens when we die?

In this worldview, your death results in the complete extinction of your consciousness, personality, and individuality. The atoms of your physical body rejoin the cosmos to be reorganized in some other way.

No hope. No meaning. No significance. No morality. (Now have a nice day!)

It's no coincidence that the genocidal murderers of the twentieth century—Hitler, Stalin, Mao, Pol Pot—were pure materialists. After all, the extermination of ten million lives here or there is of little consequence if a human is nothing more than a complex collection of elements.

And if this brief life is all one has . . . if right, wrong, and morality are meaningless, artificial inventions . . . then why shouldn't one do whatever is necessary in the name of progress?

What depressing and frightening places this worldview takes you when you begin to connect the dots. In fact, where it leads many people is to another variation on this worldview theme. It's where Klebold and Harris ended up on their way to the Columbine shootings. And it's where a huge number of America's young people live today.

POSTMODERNISM/NIHILISM: "WHATEVER" = GOD

Louis B. Mayer was the second *M* in the famed MGM Studio empire. He presided over Metro-Goldwyn-Mayer through Hollywood's golden age and was the architect of the powerful studio system that made stars of Clark Gable, Spencer Tracy, Katharine Hepburn, Judy Garland, and many others.

Mayer lived as one of the most powerful and influential men in America. In fact, he was the first corporate executive in America to earn a million-dollar salary. He was, by most reports, a decent man who enjoyed a life of remarkable wealth, prestige, and influence. Yet it was reported that, on his deathbed, his final words on this earth were, "Nothing matters. Nothing matters."[18]

We can't know what Mayer meant when he breathed those words, but they capture perfectly the essence of the related worldviews of postmodernism and nihilism.

The word *postmodernism* obviously implies that we are *post* (or beyond) the era of *modernism*. The modernism referred to is that brief period of rapid innovation and discovery at the end of the nineteenth century and the beginning of the twentieth. It was a time in which it seemed that science and reason would solve every problem, overcome every challenge, and make heaven on earth possible. It is characterized by an earnest, optimistic faith in the "inevitability of progress." That was before two world wars and the advent of atomic weapons turned most intellectuals into pessimists.

Postmodern thinking is generally characterized by these two related assumptions:

1. It is impossible to know what is "true." Neither religion nor science has the ability to tell you what is real or right. We can't "know" anything with certainty.
2. Logic and reason can lead you only to what is true *for you*. You can't impose your truth on anyone else. All truth is relative, and no person's truth is superior to another's.

While there are other common aspects to postmodern thinking, it's easy to predict how this worldview will answer the questions: What is really real? and What is the nature of the world around us?

The postmodernist's answers are, respectively: "We don't know," and "We can't know."

This is why you frequently hear postmodernists label people who hold a biblical worldview "intolerant." The Christian (at least the Christian who thinks like one) can't and won't buy into postmodernism's fundamental presuppositions.

Postmodern thought has so completely infused the world of academics and education that even the subject of mathematics has been corrupted. To most of us, it seems that the expression $2 + 3 = 5$ should not be controversial. It is objectively "true." But not to the postmodernist. Such a preoccupation with "right" answers is out of bounds. As a result, many schoolchildren today are taught a postmodern view of math. A teacher's guide to a widely used textbook for middle school students encourages teachers to point out that "mathematics is man-made, that it is arbitrary, and good solutions are arrived at by consensus among those who are considered expert."[19]

As Nancy Pearcey observed about this trend:

[I]f math is arbitrary, then there are no wrong answers, just different perspectives. In Minnesota teachers are instructed to be tolerant of "multiple mathematical worldviews." In New Mexico, I met a young man who had recently graduated from high school, where a mathematics teacher had labeled him a "bigot" for thinking it was important to get the right answer. As long as students worked together in a group and achieved consensus, the teacher insisted, the outcome was acceptable.[20]

The Bible speaks to this sort of reasoning in Romans chapter 1, verse 22: "Professing themselves to be wise, they became fools . . ." It would be a foolish person indeed that would subscribe to this sort of vain babbling.

Let me ask you, would you want to drive across a new bridge designed by an engineer trained in postmodern math? I wouldn't, either.

The postmodern train of thought has a permanent stop at the end of the line. It's a dark place called nihilism. The *American Heritage Dictionary* defines *nihilism* in this way:

1. (a) An extreme form of skepticism that denies all existence.
   (b) A doctrine holding that all values are baseless and that nothing can be known or communicated.
2. Rejection of all distinctions in moral or religious value and a willingness to repudiate all previous theories of morality or religious belief.[21]

Selfish and self-destructive lifestyles are the order of the day when this worldview is embraced. It's no wonder that the norm among teenagers today is to have as many sex partners as possible in the shortest amount of time and to engage in other risky behaviors. After all, this life is all there is, and who's to say anything is wrong or bad?

When Perry Farrell, the lead singer of the "grunge" band Porno for Pyros, sings: "Ain't no wrong, ain't no right, only pleasure and pain," he is articulating the nihilist position. Fellow grunge rocker Kurt Cobain—the voice of Generation X—followed nihilism to its logical conclusion. He had experienced hedonistic pleasure and found it utterly empty. Tired of the pain, he put a shotgun to his head in 1994.[22]

There is a reason why *Seinfeld*, a self-proclaimed "show about nothing," was enormously popular in the 1990s. And there's a reason why the last few generations, fully vested with a postmodern/nihilist worldview, have come up with a universal reply to any confident assertion of truth or fact . . .

"Whatever."

NEW AGE MONISM/PANTHEISM: EVERYTHING = GOD

In one ditch you have the atheistic worldviews of humanism, naturalism, and postmodernism—declaring God does not exist, or if He does, He is unknowable. On the opposite side of the road of truth, you'll find the ditch of monism and pantheism.

Monistic religions and philosophies (e.g., Hinduism, Buddhism, and many of the current flavors of New Age mysticism) assert that God is *in* everything and that, in fact, God *is* everything. All matter, energy, spirit, and everything composed of these elements are simply part of a cosmic Oneness.

Pantheism, the belief in many gods, is embodied in many of the popular new cults of paganism, Wicca (witchcraft), goddess worship, and the occult. At 65 percent with biblical morals, we had *Casper the Friendly Ghost*; at 35 percent, we had *Nightmare on Elm Street*; who can imagine what kinds of nightmares will come with only 4 percent espousing biblical morality? The counterculture movements of the 1960s accelerated America's infatuation with Eastern mysticism. The Beatles' very public dabbling in the teachings of the Maharishi Mahesh Yogi helped throw open the floodgates of Eastern religious ideas, assumptions, and practices in the West. All of these have allowed people to feel very trendy and "spiritual" without the calls to service, sacrifice, and humility demanded by following Christ.

Today's popular culture has fully integrated many of these Eastern concepts without questioning the origins or the implications. As in the Sheryl Crow example at the beginning of this chapter, people speak of karma in casual conversation, and the listener invariably understands what is meant. Transcendental meditation and yoga are widely practiced. And millions now arrange their furniture—and even the orientation of their newly constructed homes—in accordance with the Chinese-Taoist principles of Feng Shui (pronounced fung shway). If you're trying to sell your home in trendy California, heaven help you if your house faces the wrong direction according to Feng Shui dictates!

Keep in mind that every civilization and culture is a product of its worldview assumptions. So, ask yourself: How many of today's proponents and practitioners of Eastern religion would care to actually live in any of those nations that monism or pantheism has produced? Precious few, I can assure you.

As I've stated, most suffering in the world today stems from war, bad government, or bad religion. And most of those disastrous, bad religions are monistic or pantheistic in nature. In truth, the millions of Americans who have embraced New Age mysticism want to have their cake and eat it too. They arrogantly expect to enjoy the blessings of living in a civilization built upon Judeo-Christian assumptions, while simultaneously despising those assumptions and embracing their opposites.

Finally, it's important to note one other presupposition common to most Eastern and New Age worldviews—the cyclical nature of life and history. From the Eastern perspective, the universe is on a merry-go-round, not a path.

With that in mind, you'll recall that James Sire's seventh worldview question was: What is the meaning of human history? As we'll see in the coming pages, the way a civilization answers that question has massive implications.

ACTION POINTS

- Recognize that everyone (you included) has a worldview. The only question is: What assumptions or "presuppositions" is it built upon? (And are those assumptions true?)
- As you read magazines, watch television, view movies and converse with others, be on the lookout for worldview clues. Learn to recognize Humanist, Marxist, Materialist, New Age, and Postmodernist worldviews in the assertions presented to you.
- Recognize the idolatry inherent in false worldviews, e.g., Man = God, The State = God, etc.. Then support organizations that endeavor to educate believers, particularly young Christians, about the deceptive nature of false worldviews.
- Visit www.victimsofcommunism.org and acquaint yourself with the horrific historical facts about the most murderous worldview in human history.
- Suggested reading:

How Now Shall We Live?, by Charles Colson and Nancy Pearcey[23]

Truth Decay: Defending Christianity Against the Challenges of Postmodernism, by Douglas R. Groothius[24]

The Universe Next Door, by James W. Sire[25]

four

THE REAL THING

I hope you'll not allow yourself to be put off by the fact that we are covering a lot of philosophical ground in a short space.

Please understand, I'm not trying to turn you into a philosopher. I do hope to inspire you to be a force for restoration in our culture. I have no interest in your becoming a history professor, but I do have a passion for helping you become a formidable advocate for truth. That same desire compelled me to launch the Center for Moral Clarity in 2004 (www.centerformoralclarity.net), and it has been something I've tried to impart to the 12,000-member-and-growing congregation it is my privilege to lead at World Harvest Church in Columbus, Ohio, as well as to the audience of our *Breakthrough* media ministries.

As I stated previously, one of the main reasons the evangelical church is faring so poorly in the current clash of cultures is that so few followers of Christ actually have a fully biblical worldview. The majority of believers today carry around a hodgepodge of biblical and nonbiblical assumptions. We've retained a core of biblical presuppositions while uncritically picking up others from the dominant antibiblical culture.

Before we can successfully engage the culture and contend for the faith, we're going to have to be prepared to do more than just share the Four Spiritual Laws (though too few can do even that!). We must be equipped to think clearly and biblically. As Chuck Colson has said, Christians are to be "agents of God's *saving grace*—bringing others to Christ . . . But we are also agents of His *common grace*: We're to sustain and renew His creation, defend the created institutions of family and society, and critique false worldviews."[1]

I will take a pen and paper, a laptop computer and printer, a microphone or megaphone, or a plexiglass pulpit in a cathedral or a soapbox on a street corner and shout if I must to provoke us to become agents of common grace. This necessarily begins with an understanding that biblical truth speaks to every area of human activity—not just "church life" and private "spirituality." This is why I become uncomfortable at the everyday usage of spiritual vernacular such as "sanctuary", which has come to mean a place where Christians hide out from the "evil world"; and "services" where everything but actual service happens. Becoming an agent of common grace also means understanding that we haven't preached the "whole" gospel to our culture until we have made a compelling case for God's revealed principles in every one of those "institutions of family and society" mentioned by Colson.

You've had a brief introduction to the pretenders and contenders that are vying for the minds of Americans. Now it's time to ask: Just what are the presuppositions of a thoroughly Christian worldview?

I could write twenty volumes to answer that question (and some have). But the fact is, you can find the entirety of a biblical worldview in the simple, familiar words of Hebrews 11:6:

> But without faith it is impossible to please Him, for he who comes to God must believe that **He is**, and that **He is a rewarder** of those who diligently seek Him. (emphasis added)

The two bedrock piers that support the foundation of a Christian worldview are found in the last half of that verse. "He [God] is . . . ," and He is "a rewarder" of those who seek Him. He is a father to the orphan, a husband to the widow, and a friend to the sojourner from a far country. To those that walk in darkness, He is the Bright and Morning Star. To those who pass through the valley of the shadow of death, He is the Lily of the Valley and the Rose of Sharon. He is bread to those who are hungry and water to those who are thirsty. He is honey in the rock, a river in the wilderness and a spring of refreshing in the burning desert. Best of all, He *is*, not just was or will be—He *is* right now!

In other words:

1. God exists—He created the physical universe. Though He is present in creation, He is separate from and stands outside of creation.
2. He is knowable—What He desires and expects from us can be known—primarily through His revealed Word, but secondarily through His creation.

The theologian Carl F. H. Henry had this in mind when he wrote: "[E]vangelical theology dares harbor one and only one presupposition: the living and personal God intelligibly known in His revelation."[2] It is telling that all of the nonbiblical worldviews categorically reject one or both of these fundamental truths. I need to say it again: God exists, and He is knowable.

Others, such as Charles Colson and Nancy Pearcey, have boiled the Christian worldview down to a simple three-part grid of truth: (1) creation, (2) the fall, and (3) redemption.

For example, biblical Christians embrace the simple declaration of Genesis 1:1, which states, "In the beginning God created the heavens and the earth." And they concur with the "twenty-four elders" in the book of Revelation who fall down before the throne of God and cry, "You are worthy, O Lord, / To receive glory and honor and power; / **For You created all things, / And by Your will they exist and were created**" (Revelation 4:11, emphasis added). From beginning to end, God's Word reveals that we are part of a *creation* that is the handiwork of a *Creator*.

Second, the Bible's revelation of the fall enables Christians to make sense of the world. The puzzles of human depravity, universal suffering, and natural calamities are suddenly solved the moment you understand the implications of what God's Word describes in the second and third chapters of Genesis.

The fall of man explains the spiritual hunger that resides in every person—Blaise Pascal's "God-shaped void" that clearly lies within us all.

Third, the Bible's magnificent, front-to-back story of God's unfolding plan to redeem lost man and a fallen world gives the Christian an understanding of his place in the cosmos as well as the keys to making things whole and good again. It is fascinating to me to note that the Bible uses only three pages to describe the creation of the universe and everything in it, including the life of our pristine parents in the Garden of Eden and the fall. The Bible then devotes 1163 pages to the magnificent story of redemption—getting us back to where we started, in intimate fellowship with God through Christ.

What is more, these three pillars of truth—creation, the fall, and redemption—also give biblical Christians a framework for recognizing the fallacies and false assumptions of competing worldviews. As Nancy Pearcey explains in her book *Total Truth*:

[E]very philosophy or ideology has to answer the same fundamental questions:

1. CREATION: How did it all begin? Where did we come from?
2. FALL: What went wrong? What is the source of evil and suffering?
3. REDEMPTION: What can we do about it? How can the world be set right again?[3]

As we have seen, and will continue to see through the balance of this work, only biblical Christianity brings meaningful, coherent, and tested answers to these most basic questions.

GOING DEEPER

Of course, these three pillars of a biblical worldview can easily be unpacked so as to answer the seven key questions outlined by James Sire in the previous chapter.

I want to give some attention to each of these. Why? Because making sure you have the Bible's supernaturally revealed answers to each of these questions is the best way to know your worldview hasn't been compromised by any elements from the false paradigms that bombard us each day in this media-saturated world.

1. WHAT IS PRIME REALITY—THE REALLY REAL?

As the Bible makes clear, the prime reality is God Himself. I think it is significant that the Gospel of John starts with the same three words as does Genesis—"In the beginning . . ."

In Genesis, God, through Moses, begins the orientation process for His covenant people by explaining prime reality to them: "In the beginning God created the heavens and the earth." In the Book of John, God initiates the orientation process for His "new covenant" people in precisely the same way:

> In the beginning was the Word, and the Word was with God, and the Word was God. (John 1:1)

James Sire has written that the Bible's answer to this question of "prime reality" can be summarized this way: "God is infinite and personal (triune), transcendent and immanent, omniscient, sovereign and good." This is as concise a description of God as I've ever seen. Of course, each word is laden with meaning and significance.

Let me address two of them that may not be widely understood—*transcendent* and *immanent*.

Transcendence and immanence refer to the dual truths that, though God is *present* in creation, He is separate and distinct from it. This stands in stark contrast to the false view of the monistic, Eastern religions we examined in the previous chapter. In those belief systems, God, or a life force of some sort, is broken up into fragments that make up the universe. Thus, God isn't just present in creation; He is creation. God is in you, and God *is* you.

When in the Bible, God says, "I am holy," He is declaring His transcendence—His "otherness" or separateness from creation. When He says, "I, the Lord your God, am with you," He is proclaiming His immanence.

2. WHAT IS THE NATURE OF EXTERNAL REALITY, THAT IS, THE WORLD AROUND US?

The Bible's response to this question is to assert that God created the universe, and that He made it *ex nihilo*, or "out of nothing." In the words of Hebrews 11:3: "The things which are seen were not made of things which are visible."

This astonishing and straightforward declaration is strikingly different from the elaborate creation myths of ancient cultures.

For example, the Egyptians believed the world was created by Atum, who appeared as a hill out of the waters of chaos and then mated with his shadow to create offspring. In the Babylonian creation story of Enuma Elish, the demi-god Marduk battles the goddess Tiamat, defeats her, and then cuts her into two pieces, which become the sky and the subterranean waters. The ancient Chinese story of creation involves a being named P'an Ku who grows inside a giant egg containing all the elements of the universe. After eighteen thousand years, the egg is hatched, P'an Ku dies, but his eyes become the sun and moon. Certain Native American creation stories depict the earth resting on a turtle's back.

Contrast those colorful tales with the Bible's simple assertion that a personal pre-existent, all-powerful, eternal God spoke, and the universe began. And not only was God the cause of and force behind creation—the Bible also tells us that He created it orderly and predictable.

As we've seen in previous chapters, this understanding (or a rejection of it) carries huge implications. They will become even more apparent in the chapters to come.

3. WHAT IS A HUMAN BEING?

I like the way Francis Schaeffer answered that question in his book *Escape from Reason*. He wrote: "God tells man who he is. God tells us that He created man in His image. So man is something wonderful."[4]

This is the middle-road of truth between the false extremes of humanism and materialism. To the humanist, the human being is everything, and "human potential" is messiah. To the materialist, human beings are nothing. Just an accident of evolution that resulted from the prior accident of the emergence of life, which was, in turn, an accident of the formation of the universe around certain physical laws following the Big Bang.

G. K. Chesterton had the materialist view of man in his crosshairs when he fired this shot:

> It is not natural to see man as a natural product, it is not seeing straight to see him as an animal. It is not sane. It sins against the light, against the broad daylight of proportion, which is the principle of all reality.[5]

The Bible makes two significant assertions about humanity. The first is that God made man "in His image and likeness." In fact, the point is emphasized three times in the space of two verses in Genesis:

> Then God said, "Let Us make man **in Our image**, according to Our likeness; let them have dominion over the fish of the sea, over the birds of the air, and over the cattle, over all the earth and over every creeping thing that creeps on the earth." **So God created man in His own image; in the image of God He created him**; male and female He created them. (Genesis 1:26–27, emphasis added)

The Bible's second major assertion about man is that he was created "a little lower than the angels" [The Hebrew word translated "angels" here is "elohim" and is translated "God" elsewhere] (Psalm 45:6–7; Psalm 104:1).

The Bible's clear message is that man was the crowning glory of creation. And furthermore, the rest of nature was placed here for man's use, stewardship, and enjoyment. Look at the above-cited passage in Psalms in context:

When I consider Your heavens, the work of Your fingers,
The moon and the stars, which You have ordained,
What is man that You are mindful of him,
And the son of man that You visit him?
For You have made him a little lower than the angels
And You have crowned him with glory and honor.
You have made him to have dominion over the works of Your hands;
You have put all things under his feet,
All sheep and oxen—
Even the beasts of the field,
The birds of the air,
And the fish of the sea
That pass through the paths of the seas. (Psalm 8:3–8)

How utterly different this paradigm is from the naturalist view described in the previous chapter—where people are viewed as a destructive scourge upon the otherwise pristine Planet Earth. Spend a little time reading much of the militant environmentalist literature and you'll quickly get the impression the writers believe "Mother Earth" would be much better off if humans disappeared tomorrow. And ironically, it has been humanists at the forefront of promoting abortion and euthanasia under the banner of "quality of life" concerns.

Of this, Francis Schaeffer wrote:

We must understand that the question of the dignity of human life is not something on the periphery of Judeo-Christian thinking, but almost in the center of it (though not *the* center because the center is the existence of God Himself). It is because there is a personal-infinite God who has made men and women in His own image that they have a unique dignity of life as human beings.[6]

Thus, Christianity as revealed through God's Word dares to make some bold assertions that are almost considered blasphemy according to current pop culture orthodoxy. Among them:

- People are vastly more important than animals. (But the Bible charges us with avoiding cruelty toward the animals we use.)
- It is right to utilize nature and natural resources for the benefit of humans. (But we are also charged with wise stewardship responsibilities over nature and toward future generations of humans.)

This is precisely why we, at the Center for Moral Clarity, fought so tirelessly during the session of the 108th Congress to marshal grassroots support for legislation such as the Partial Birth Abortion Ban Act, the Unborn Victims of Violence Act, and prohibitions on the patenting of humans at every stage of life.

Of course, as I have noted, one of the key elements in making biblical sense of the world is recognizing that the fall impacted everything. Man's original disobedience unleashed powerful forces of destruction and decay upon the earth. The image of God in man was marred and twisted.

What are the value and the place of man in God's eyes? How should we view our fellow human beings? The apostle John pointed us toward an answer when God prompted him to write: "This is love: not that we loved God, but that he loved us and sent his Son as an atoning sacrifice for our sins. Dear friends, since God so loved us, we also ought to love one another" (1 John 4:10–11 NIV).

4. What happens to a person at death?

Until very recently, a belief in life after death was nearly universal on earth. In every place and in every time, it has run counter to common

71

sense and intuition to think that individual human consciousness is extinguished by death. It also runs counter to the clear teaching of Scripture.

In Jesus' time, the Sadducees were one of those rare groups, like today's materialists, who denied the possibility of life after death. Jesus rejected this view and taught clearly and consistently that the soul was eternal and persistent. Even as He hung on the cross, He promised the repentant, dying thief beside Him, "Today you will be with me in paradise" (Luke 23:43).

James Sire describes the biblical view of human death this way:

> For each person death is either the gate to life with God and his people or the gate to eternal separation from the only thing that will ultimately fulfill human aspirations.[7]

It's important to note at this point that the Hindu concept of reincarnation is absolutely incompatible and irreconcilable with biblical revelation. The Bible is clear and consistent: "As it is appointed for men to die once, but after this the judgment" (Hebrews 9:27).

It is a mystery—but one a child can grasp. As the Scots preacher Alexander MacLaren once said, "I know what Eternity is, though I cannot define the word to satisfy a metaphysician. The little child taught by some grandmother Lois, in a cottage, knows what she means when she tells him, 'you will live forever,' though both scholar and teacher would be puzzled to put it into other words."[8]

I received an understanding of living forever as an eight-year-old boy. Glimpsing eternity, my fallen condition, and a heavenly Father's sacrificial love, I bowed my knee and embraced His gift of life in Christ. I can tell you, nothing for me has ever been the same.

5. WHY IS IT POSSIBLE TO KNOW ANYTHING AT ALL?

There is a fancy academic word used to identify the issues surrounding different theories of *knowing*. It is *epistemology*. Believe it or not, countless volumes have been written and huge debates have raged across the centuries about just *what* it is we can actually know and *how* we can know it.

When we start with the assumption that God exists (contrary to the claims of humanism and naturalism), and that He exists outside of and distinct from creation (contrary to the claims of Eastern mysticism and New Age thought), the Christian stands on solid, confident ground on the question of what we can truly know.

For the Christian, God is the ultimate reality. He is eternal and unchanging in character. And because He has chosen to reveal Himself through creation, through supernaturally inspired Scripture, and ultimately through the incarnation of Himself in Jesus Christ— we can know things with certainty. This is not the case with nonbiblical worldviews.

Without an "everlasting Father" standing behind creation, other worldviews find themselves in a dark night and on ever-shifting sand—with no solid ground upon which to stand.

The humanist claims knowledge is purely the product of human experience. We know, however, that since man is fallen and flawed, human experience alone is unreliable.

The materialist starts with the assumption that the human mind and self-awareness are just accidents of physics. Therefore, everything we think we know is suspect and subject to revision when a "better theory" comes along.

And the holders of postmodern and New Age worldviews embrace relativism, which claims that "all things are true and in a constant state of flux . . . there is no objective truth: anything which a person can perceive is true for that person, but not necessarily true for the next person."[9]

In stunning contrast, the biblical believer stands on rock-solid ground in bright light. We declare, with the psalmist, "Your word is a lamp to my feet / And a light to my path" (Psalm 119:105). We agree with John, who said of the Word (Jesus): "In Him was life, and the life was the light of men." (John 1:4) And that Jesus was a perfect representation of the Father's character and nature, according to

Hebrews 1:2–3. Let us therefore declare with Job, whose words are recorded in the oldest book in the Bible, "For I know that my Redeemer lives . . ." (Job 19:25)

6. HOW DO WE KNOW WHAT IS RIGHT AND WRONG?

The humanist, the materialist, and the Eastern mystic all find themselves in agreement about *ethics*, that is, issues relating to what is right and wrong. All will tell you that there are no moral absolutes . . . no unchanging standards of right and wrong . . . and of course, no sin.

Now, people who hold these worldviews will certainly talk about certain things being "right" or "good" and other things being "wrong" or "evil." But when they are pressed to identify the basis or source of these designations, you won't get a clear answer. They borrow the language of morality but deny any basis for it. Some will appeal to human reason. Others will offer practical arguments—saying things are "right" because they seem to work.

But for the holder of a biblical worldview, right and wrong have nothing to do with what we think, feel, observe, or figure out. God's existence, character, and revealed will are the only ultimate reality and are therefore the standard by which everything can and must be measured.

Therefore, as James Sire has written, "[E]thics, while very much a human domain, is ultimately the business of God. We are not the measure of morality. God is."[10] This is the biblical view.

7. WHAT IS THE MEANING OF HUMAN HISTORY?

For most of us *history* is the name of a subject we were required to take in school—and for many a boring one at that. But in a discussion of worldviews, the term *history* refers to much more than just the record of past names and dates. It speaks of the unfolding course of human events past, present, and future. Not surprisingly, different worldviews have radically differing interpretations of what history means.

Of course, the Bible presents God as the Author and Lord of history. Immediately after the fall of man in Genesis, we find God indicating that He had a plan of redemption that would unfold. In Genesis 3, God lets Adam and Eve know the implications of the curses they have unleashed upon the earth and upon their descendants. Then, in pronouncing a curse upon the serpent, God says:

And I will put enmity
Between you and the woman,
And between your seed and her Seed;
He shall bruise your head,
And you shall bruise His heel.

Here God begins the "scarlet thread of redemption" that He weaves through the whole tapestry of Scripture. He decrees a future day in which a "Seed" (singular) of the woman will crush the head of the serpent. In scores of other Scriptures, God shows that He is steering history toward a predetermined end of His choosing. And though He has given individuals free will—John Ashcroft said, "God valued choice so much in all of us that when He created us, He even allowed us to choose against God"[11] and therefore the option of embracing or rejecting His good plan for their own lives—no individual, group, or nation can thwart His plan for mankind. History is moving toward a resolution of God's own design.

What peace this affords us. The famous gospel song *Because He Lives* is a well-known affirmation of this great hope for the future.

This, of course, stands in sharp contrast to the way competing worldviews approach man's unfolding story.

Humanist Manifesto I was full of optimism and faith in the inevitability of human progress. But World War II and the Cold War had put a serious damper on humanist enthusiasm by the time Humanist Manifesto II was written in the 1970s. To the naturalists and materialists, history clearly can have no meaning, because everything we see, think, and know is just the product of random chance.

And what of the nihilist view of history?

A telling piece of dialogue in the 2005 horror movie *Constantine*—a theologically confused story about demons and angels and their attempts to influence man—encapsulates nihilism's take. A female character expresses her faith by saying, "I know God has a plan for me." The cynical, burned-out title character, Constantine, bursts her bubble with his nihilist worldview in a nutshell. He wearily tells her: "God is a kid with an ant farm. There is no plan."

That characterization is tragically wrong on several levels. Of course, there is a plan—a wonderful one. What comfort and strength the Christian can take from the knowledge that a sovereign, heavenly Father is actively moving history toward a glorious end of His choosing. In His own words:

> I am God, and there is none like Me,
> Declaring the end from the beginning,
> And from ancient times things that are not yet done,
> Saying, "My counsel shall stand,
> And I will do all My pleasure." (Isaiah 46:9–10)

Yes, He will. Of course, that doesn't mean the enemy hasn't been active throughout history deceiving as many people as possible with seductive lies. As we'll see in the coming pages, though the author of false worldviews made his destructive debut in the Garden of Eden, he was only getting warmed up.

NOW WHAT?

I opened this chapter by letting you know I wasn't trying to turn you into a philosophy professor, but rather a force for cultural change. This brings us to an eighth and vital element of a thoroughly biblical worldview.

You see, it's not enough to simply say "Yes!" and "Amen!" to the seven key assumptions I've laid out above. It's not even enough to be able to discern how other worldviews are wrong and/or destructive. Those things are important, but we must also *do* something with that knowledge. If we don't stop playing church, get outside the four walls of the sanctuary, and begin modeling the compassion of Christ toward a hurting world, we're going to lose this nation. We have to take the biblical truth we know and start applying it in the statehouse, the schoolhouse, and the marketplace. As the book of James tells us, "Faith without works is dead." Thus, we must move beyond *thinking* right and start *doing* right.

This division between the secular and the spiritual, which so many Christians carry around today, is an artificial one. It is a distinction that is completely foreign to the thinking of Jesus, Paul, or the founders of our nation. In fact, it is a pagan, gnostic heresy that the apostle John spent much effort to refute.

Jesus told His disciples to pray to the Father: "Your kingdom come. Your will be done on earth as it is in heaven" (Matthew 6:10). To paraphrase in modern language, "Lord, extend and expand Your rule so that things here on earth get done Your way, just as they are in heaven!" Paul spoke in military terms about "casting down arguments and every high thing that exalts itself against the knowledge of God, bringing every thought into captivity to the obedience of Christ" (2 Corinthians 10:5).

To the believer, everything is sacred. Everything we touch is a candidate for redemption and renewal through the bringing of God's light and truth to it. And we neglect our responsibilities as kingdom ambassadors when we fail to carry that light and truth into every realm of human endeavor.

As the previous pages have begun to demonstrate, the Bible is more than just a guide for clean living. It speaks powerfully and authoritatively to the realms of economics, art, entertainment, and government. And as the pages that follow will show, every thorny public policy issue of our time can be illuminated by the wisdom of applied biblical truth. From medical ethics to the environment, from taxation and poverty to war—the holder of a biblical worldview brings practical, workable parameters for righteous policies. But that's just it. We must *bring* them. That is why we also have to bury, once and forever, the old myth that Christians must set their faith aside when they engage the broader culture which includes the world of politics or, better yet, avoid it altogether. It is more than a myth. It is a prescription for cultural death and decay. We should not and must not apologize for bringing a robust biblical perspective into the voting booth and into public policy debates. Too much is at stake. Too many innocent lives hang in the balance. Too many freedoms are in jeopardy.

By some estimates, more than four million Christians sat out the ultra-close and hotly disputed presidential election of 2000.[12] If that number had been any larger, the election would surely have swung a different direction, with disastrous consequences for our nation in my opinion. Four years later, Christians clearly made a difference, but far too many still remained spectators in this battle for our culture rather than joining the fight.

I will outline a biblical strategy for cultural and political engagement in Chapter 11. For now, I want you to recognize that worldview is vitally important, but only as a foundation for equipping a mighty force for redemption, restoration, and renewal in America.

As you're about to see, we don't have a moment to waste.

ACTION POINTS

- Purpose to become "a force for restoration in our culture." Absorb the truths in books like this one and begin to contend for the truth of the Christian worldview.
- Embrace God's view of Man—that we are special, the crowning glory of Creation, yet fallen and in need of redemption.
- Support public policies, legislation and state constitutional amendments that protect human life, including bans on partial birth abortion, therapeutic cloning, and embryonic stem cell research.
- Make sure you have personally accepted God's provision for redeeming fallen Man—His Son, Jesus Christ.
- Get outside the four walls of the sanctuary, and begin modeling the compassion of Christ toward a hurting world. Work with others to bring relief to the poor and oppressed in the name of Christ.
- Visit The Center for Moral Clarity Web site at www.centerformoralclarity.net and learn specific steps you can take to contend for the truth in our nation.
- Suggested reading:

Idols for Destruction: The Conflict of Christian Faith and American Culture, by Herbert Schlossberg[13]
Making the Connections: How to Put Biblical Worldview Integration into Practice, by Christian Overman[14]
Understanding the Times: The Religious Worldviews of Our Day and the Search for Truth, by David Noebel[15]
The Victory of Reason: How Christianity Led to Freedom, Capitalism, and Western Success, by Rodney Stark[16]

five

THE FATHERS OF FALSEHOOD:
THE ROOTS OF THE CURRENT CONFLICT

John Adams was dying—and he knew it. At ninety years of age and desperately ill, the man who was our nation's second president had been fighting fiercely for weeks just to hang on. He clung tenaciously to life because, as he made clear to those caring for him, he had prayed fervently that God would not call him home before this special day.

The day was July 4, 1826—the fiftieth anniversary of the signing of the Declaration of Independence. You see, Adams was the man who, second only to Thomas Jefferson, was most responsible for the ideas and words of that world-changing document. Adams, like Jefferson, considered the drafting of the Declaration to be the most significant contribution in his long, distinguished career.

At some point that afternoon, knowing he had lived to see that milestone anniversary, Adams opened his eyes, whispered, "Thomas Jefferson still survives," and slipped into eternity. But he was mistaken. Jefferson had died just a few hours earlier at the age of eighty-three.

Many historians have marveled at the extraordinary coincidence that both these men who had such an influence on our nation's founding would die on the same day and upon one so special to both of them. Throughout the course of their long, history-making lives they had at various times been co-revolutionaries, bitter political opponents, correspondents, and friends. But the two men were something more. As David McCullough highlights in his excellent biography of Adams, the two men "had in common a love for books and ideas but differed on almost every other imaginable point."[1]

Indeed, they are representatives of two worldviews that fought for inclusion and supremacy as the laws and institutions of our embryonic nation were being forged—biblical Christianity and rationalistic Deism.

John Adams was a real-deal Christian. And, unlike many believers today, he had a fully developed biblical worldview. Though recently some academics have made weak attempts to paint Adams as anti-Christian, they do so by pointing to instances in which, late in life, he took certain religious clergymen to task for failing to follow biblical principles. I must tell you, if doing that makes a person anti-Christian, then this preacher is in trouble. I have taken other clergy to task, for example, for excusing abortion because of poverty, and I've done it on national television. No, Adams deeply and sincerely believed that God, as He revealed Himself in the Bible, was real, sovereign, and active in the affairs of men and nations. His personal correspondence gives us the clearest view into his soul, as in this letter to his wife, Abigail, written on the eve of war with mighty Britain:

> I feel no anxiety at the large armament designed against us. The remarkable interpositions of heaven in our favor cannot be too gratefully acknowledged. He who fed the Israelites in the wilderness, who clothes the lilies of the field and who feeds the young ravens when they cry, will not forsake a people engaged in so righteous a cause, if we remember His loving kindness.[2]

We get a little insight into both Adams's faith and his sentiment about the date of the signing of the Declaration, when he says of July Fourth: "It ought to be commemorated, as the Day of Deliverance, by solemn acts of devotion to God Almighty."[3]

Like that of a number of his fellow founders, and many of his countrymen living in the American colonies in the eighteenth century, John Adams's faith was solid and Bible-based. I suspect there is not one position among the eight biblical worldview points I described in the previous chapter to which Adams would not have given hearty assent. That's why, late in life, we find him writing this to his old political adversary, Thomas Jefferson:

> The general principles upon which the Fathers achieved independence were the general principles of Christianity . . . I will avow that I believed and now believe that those general principles of Christianity are as eternal and immutable as the existence and the attributes of God.[4]

Similar words were unlikely to flow from the gifted pen of Thomas Jefferson. The writings of the man whose letter to the Danbury Baptist Association gave us the expression "separation of church and state"—the concept recent courts have used as a lever for prying vestiges of the Christian faith from the public square—reveal a very different worldview.

It is a worldview that grudgingly acknowledges the existence of a Creator-God but denies that He is in any way active in His creation. It therefore categorically denies the divinity of Jesus Christ. This philosophy views the universe as a complex clockwork mechanism, wound up by God at the beginning of time, and then simply left to run on its own. This is not many steps removed from the "God is a kid with an ant farm" theology espoused by the character in the movie *Constantine*.

There is a name for this worldview. It is Deism.

Dr. D. James Kennedy and others have correctly pointed out that modern atheists and humanists have exaggerated Thomas Jefferson's Deism to advance their agendas and to refute claims that America was founded as a Christian nation.[5] But it is difficult to deny that Jefferson exalted human reason and doubted the possibility of divine revelation—two key pillars of Deist thought. Nor is it possible to deny that a good many others of his day had been seduced by aspects of Deism, including George Washington, Benjamin Franklin, and Thomas Paine (though Franklin clearly abandoned his Deism in his later years).

Paine was perhaps the most vocal and militant Deist of his day. Paine's fiery, pro-independence pamphlet, *Common Sense*, was clearly instrumental in galvanizing support for the Revolutionary War. But more quietly influential was his book *The Age of Reason*, which laid out the intellectual case for Deism. It was highly skeptical of religion and of the Bible. In it, Paine wrote: "[I]t would be more consistent that we called it the word of a demon, than the Word of God. It is a history of wickedness, that has served to corrupt and brutalize mankind; and, for my own part, I sincerely detest it, as I detest everything that is cruel."[6]

He captured the "rationalist" spirit of the Deists when he wrote: "My own mind is my own church. All national institutions of churches, whether Jewish, Christian or Turkish, appear to me no other than human inventions, set up to terrify and enslave mankind, and monopolize power and profit." Paine frequently wrote passionately and worshipfully of Reason (with a capital *R*) as if human intellect were almost a divine force.

Yet at the very same time, there were many committed, biblical Christians among our nation's founders. Among the fifty-five Founding Fathers, twenty-eight were Episcopalians, eight were Presbyterians, seven were Congregationalists, two were Lutheran, two were Dutch Reformed, two were Methodist, two were Roman Catholic, one is unknown, and only three identified themselves as Deists—Williamson, Wilson, and Franklin.

Jefferson and others believed they could discard the Bible's claims to miracles and the supernatural, while holding on to its moral and ethical teachings—which they saw as valuable for keeping the less-educated, less-enlightened riffraff in line. He went so far as to create a version of the Gospels with all of Jesus' miracles edited out, with a view toward distributing it among the Indians. He admired Jesus' ethical teachings but found the New Testament's accounts of miracles embarrassing and superstitious.

As James Sire has noted, "As interested as the early deists were in preserving the ethical content of Christianity, they were unable to find a suitable basis for it."[7] Why was this? It was because they had jettisoned the only basis for ethics and morality—the belief in a God who is present and active and holy.

Clearly, at the time of our nation's birth, two very different sets of ideas about God, man, and history were fighting for ascendancy.

WHEAT AND TARES

When I think about the history of our country, I am reminded of the parable Jesus told about the wheat and the tares.

> The kingdom of heaven is like a man who sowed good seed in his field; but while men slept, his enemy came and sowed tares among the wheat and went his way. But when the grain had sprouted and produced a crop, then the tares also appeared. (Matthew 13:24–26)

From its very beginning, our nation was a field sown primarily with the good "wheat" seed of Christian ideas and ideals. Beginning with the first Puritan settlers and their vision of a shining "city on a hill," and carrying on through 150 years of settlement and colonization, the emerging American paradigm was a robustly biblical and thoroughly Christian one. But by the time we reach the day of Adams, Jefferson, and their fellow revolutionaries, tares are very evidently growing among the wheat. Those "tares" manifested as the Deist worldview and its religious exaltation of reason, science, and man's ability to discover all truth. Where did those "tare" seeds come from? They came from the same place as the wheat seeds. They were imported from Europe.

The seventeenth and eighteenth centuries in Europe were times of tremendous upheaval in the realm of ideas. On the one hand, you have the Reformation—a move of God propelled by the Reformers Luther, Calvin, Knox, and others. The invention of the printing press and the first translations of the Bible into the languages of the people put the Scriptures in the hands of the common man for the first time in church history.

Simultaneously, what came to be known as the Enlightenment or the Age of Reason was ascending in Europe. This meant that at the very time the Reformers were correcting, restoring, and invigorating biblical faith, many European "intellectuals" were rejecting it altogether. The rationalistic, antibiblical ideas of writers such as Voltaire, David Hume, Jean-Jacques Rousseau, and Immanuel Kant—who came to believe that reason and science would eventually banish the "superstitions" of religious faith—were picked up by key individuals like Paine, Jefferson, and Franklin as they spent significant stretches of time in France and England.

Ironically, as we'll see in the next chapter, it was the Christian worldview that made reason and science possible in the first place.

Many have commented on the stark differences between the American and French revolutions. As you may know, the French Revolution began as a movement to abolish the monarchy, but quickly spiraled out of control—characterized by bloody mob violence and an endless succession of executions at the guillotine.

What was the difference? America's revolutionaries overwhelmingly held to a biblical worldview. But by 1789, the French, saturated in and infatuated with Enlightenment thinking, had almost completely embraced the Deists' worship of reason and rejection of biblical assumptions.

As one encyclopedia article on Enlightenment philosophy puts it:

> The French Revolution, in particular, represented the Enlightenment philosophy through a violent and messianic lens . . . The desire for rationality in government led to the attempt to end the Roman Catholic Church, and indeed Christianity in France.[8]

It's not hard to see how the Enlightenment concepts that gave birth to Deism would lead to humanism, materialism, and ultimately, postmodern nihilism in modern America.

To borrow from the language of chemical dependency, Deism was the "gateway drug" for our current antibiblical worldviews. Or in the language of evolution, Deism is a "transitional form"... a missing link on our culture's journey from biblical Christianity to humanistic and materialistic despair. In other words, both humanism and naturalism are branches on Deism's "family tree."

What I want you to see is that both the "wheat" and the "tare" worldview strains that have grown up together in America came from seeds that were cultivated in Europe. So to trace fully the origins of our current war of worldviews, we must look across the Atlantic.

TWO "JOHNS" OF GENEVA

Just as the worldview conflict in revolutionary America can be seen in two men—Adams and Jefferson—the European roots of that conflict can be boiled down to the conflicting views of two key individuals. They are the two "Johns" of Geneva, Switzerland—John Calvin and Jean-Jacques Rousseau. But unlike Jefferson and Adams, the two men were not contemporaries. Calvin was born a full two hundred years before Rousseau came along.

Many modern Christians know that Calvin's name ultimately became tied to an entire school of Christian theology, namely, Calvinism. But they don't fully appreciate the contributions of John Calvin to the formation of our biblical worldview or to the worldviews of so many of the leading citizens of colonial America. In fact, the great German historian Leopold Von Ranke thoroughly studied the major influences on people of that period and proclaimed John Calvin "as the virtual founder of America."[9]

Calvin's approach to the great questions of life was fully grounded in that three-part grid I described previously—creation, the fall, and redemption. He brought these assumptions to his amazing knowledge and analysis of Greek philosophy and Catholic theology. As

University of North Carolina professor Grant Horner put it, Calvin came to understand where the philosophers were wrong by

> reading and analyzing their works and comparing them to Scripture—the ultimate standard for truth . . . Calvin observes that the philosophers' basic error is their presupposition that mankind is *not* in a state of depravity [fallen sinfulness]. One cannot understand man's *nature* apart from understanding his/her *fallen nature*—and recognizing one's own fallen nature as well.[10]

Many of the great leaders, preachers, and thinkers of the colonial era were deeply impacted by Calvin's worldview approach. Many of them were instrumental in sparking the spiritual revival in the colonies, which came to be called the Great Awakening. Among them were George Whitefield, Cotton Mather, and Jonathan Edwards. Let me define for you the conditions they faced.

It was a time of tremendous moral decline. The standards held by previous generations were eroding, leaving an ethical breach that was flooded with all kinds of vices. New agendas rushed in to fill the void created by discarded tenets of Christian faith that were regarded as outmoded and obsolete. Church membership rolls were increasing, but the spiritual temperature of many in attendance was tepid at best. Science, reason, and the seemingly unlimited human capabilities were exalted above the knowledge of God.

Reform efforts aimed at cultural leaders bore little fruit. Those in positions of power tipped their hats to religion, but paid little attention as their actions speeded the secularization of society.

Young people, cut adrift from the moorings that held their ancestors steady, found pleasure in new forms of entertainment and clandestine liaisons in out-of-the-way places. The number of unwed pregnancies soared, and time-honored traditions were overthrown.

These were the conditions prevailing in the American colonies at the close of the 1720s. Who could tell that within a decade, a culture-shaking revival would not only sweep a society, but shape a new nation?

About one hundred years after Calvin's death in Geneva, we find Rousseau in the same city, drinking deeply of the Age of Enlightenment's intoxicating mix of skepticism, atheism, and worship of reason. So powerful and pervasive is Rousseau's influence on many of today's antibiblical worldviews, he merits deeper examination. And so do the other "fathers of falsehood" who followed in his wake. So, for the balance of this chapter, we'll expose the authors of some of the biggest and most insidious lies in history. And we'll begin with Rousseau himself.

THE FATHERS OF FALSEHOOD

JEAN-JACQUES ROUSSEAU

Rousseau was born in Geneva in 1712—as the so-called Age of Reason was fully underway. His mother passed away soon after his birth, and his father would abandon him at the age of ten, leaving him in the care of an aunt and uncle. As an adult, he fathered and orphaned five illegitimate children by his mistress, leaving each one, unnamed, in the care of a notorious Paris "foundling home" (a state-run orphanage) while they were still newborns. This was customary for those who had unwanted children in the days before abortion came to prominence. Of Rousseau's systematic abandonment of his own offspring, historian Paul Johnson has said:

> Owing to the huge numbers of abandoned infants with which the orphanage had to cope, conditions within it, as Rousseau knew, were appalling. Two-thirds of the children died in the first year. Only 14 in every 100 survived to the age of seven, and of these five grew to maturity, most of them to become beggars. Rousseau was thus condemning his five children to death or at best to a life of vagabondage.
>
> In order to justify his inhuman act of handing over his children to the state, in the shape of the official orphanage, Rousseau was led to argue that the state ought to be responsible for all children, if society

was to be improved. For education was the key to any social and moral advance.[11]

Indeed, many of Rousseau's later writings would center on the power of the state to raise and train children. He believed this was superior to allowing children to be raised by parents. He was convinced the government should have the role of forming the minds of children.

As I mentioned in my book, *Silent No More*, here are some examples of what happens when we give the government control of our children's education.

"Public education in this country is a dismal failure . . . Johnny can't read, and Susie can't spell . . . Willie can't write, and Alice can't add . . . Teacher competency is down . . . Administrative effectiveness is down . . . Student advancement is down . . . Test scores are down . . . Everything to do with our public school system is down—everything, that is, except crime, drug abuse, illicit sex, and the cost to taxpayers.[12]

But Rousseau went further. He actually believed individuals should desire to be "owned" by the government. For example, he was once asked to write a model constitution for the Corsican nations. In it he had citizens required to take this oath: "I join myself, body, goods, will and all my powers, to the Corsican Nation, granting her ownership of me, of myself and all who depend on me."[13]

In Rousseau's ideal world, the state would "possess men and all their powers" and control every aspect of their existence. If that sounds a lot like many of the oppressive Communist governments that arose and fell during the twentieth century, that is no accident. They were and are direct philosophical descendants of Rousseau's ideas.

It is difficult to overstate the reach of Rousseau's influence over intellectuals and artists who followed him. Not surprisingly, one of those profoundly impacted thinkers was Karl Marx. As Paul Johnson noted: "Rousseau is notable not only because his wickedness as an individual is so clearly connected to the immorality of his state theory but because through his influence on both Hegel and Marx, he set in motion the great stream of ideas which produced the ruthless regimes of the twentieth century."

Here in the twenty-first century, many humanists, naturalists, and statists extend and expand Rousseau's legacy as they uncritically accept his radical ideas.

So, the next time you hear an elected official declare that the government needs to institute more federal programs for protecting and nurturing "our children," know that you are hearing an echo of Rousseau, and ponder whether it really takes a village, or just a family, to raise a child. Besides, shouldn't parents, not government, be responsible to raise their children?

KARL MARX

We examined the worldview called Marxism in Chapter 3. With that background in mind, let's briefly explore the life of the man whose ideas, in the words of Dave Breese, "have produced the greatest degree of social, physical, and moral ruin the world has ever known."[14]

In 1818, forty-six years after Rousseau was laid to rest in Paris, Karl Marx was born, about 250 miles to the east, in Trier, Germany. Marx's father was a nonobservant Jew who converted to Lutheranism the year before Karl was born. As a boy, Marx actually considered becoming a Lutheran minister and attended a religious preparatory school. But the Europe of Marx's youth had already begun the wholesale rejection of Christianity and was too full of radical "new" ideas for him to avoid being seduced by the writings of novelists like Rousseau and scientists like Charles Darwin.

In fact, Marx ultimately took Darwin's concept of biological evolution and applied it to the realms of economics and sociology. In Marx's funeral eulogy, his lifelong friend and collaborator, Friedrich Engels, said, "Just as Darwin discovered the law of evolution in organic nature; so Marx discovered the law of evolution in human history."[15]

Marx picked up his lifelong atheism as a student at the University of Berlin among a circle of intellectual friends who enjoyed discussing the German philosopher Hegel. Because of these influences, Marx ultimately became convinced that religious belief had to be destroyed if the kinds of changes he hoped to see brought about were going to happen. In that vein, he wrote: "Man makes religion, religion does not make man . . . The abolition of religion as the illusory happiness of the people is required for their real happiness."[16]

Like many antibiblical revolutionaries, Marx had messianic dreams. He wrote: "The philosophers have only interpreted the world . . . the point, however, is to change it." Marx became convinced that the key to changing the world was not in the realm of philosophy but in economics.

Over the years, he developed elaborate theories that predicted violent uprisings and workers' revolutions across Europe. In fact, by the time Marx settled in London in 1849, he was convinced that massive, large-scale upheavals were right around the corner. But he was wrong; it wouldn't be until the 1917 Bolshevik Revolution in Russia that the first real test of Marx's theories would begin. And as we saw in Chapter 3, when they did, people begin to suffer and die on an unprecedented scale.

It may surprise you, then, to learn that Karl Marx and I do have some things in common. I, too, have a passion to see the poor, oppressed, and exploited lifted up. And I long to see people everywhere find meaning and fulfillment in their lives. The difference is, I know those things are possible only with God and through the redemption freely offered in His Son, Jesus Christ.

And unlike Marxism's colossal historical failure to bring anything but misery to men, God's way works. I've seen it transform individuals, families, communities, and whole nations.

Marx was right about one thing. History is moving unavoidably toward a specific conclusion. It's just not the one he envisioned.

Charles Darwin

"Darwin made it possible to be an intellectually fulfilled atheist."[17] So said Richard Dawkins, the radical evolutionist who, as I pointed out in Chapter 1, has suggested that teaching children religion constitutes a form of "child abuse."

The ideas of Charles Darwin have had an immeasurable impact on the world in which you and I live. That's a pretty impressive legacy for a man whose father once told him, "You care for nothing but shooting, dogs, and rat-catching and you will be a disgrace to yourself and all your family."[18]

Today Darwin's theories have infused not only the world of science, but also sociology, economics, and even theology.

Charles Darwin was born in 1809 to a British family with a distinguished tradition in science and medicine. Like Karl Marx, Darwin studied for the ministry for a time. And like Marx, he lost many vestiges of a Christian faith in the heady atmosphere of university—as he dove headfirst into Enlightenment thinking at Cambridge.

To be fair, nothing in Darwin's early writings or correspondence indicates that he aimed to undermine confidence in the Bible or belief in God. In fact, he seemed to be genuinely perplexed and dismayed by the furor his theories sparked in religious circles. And it was not Darwin, but others like British biologist Thomas Huxley—known as "Darwin's Bulldog"—who took his theories and launched a crusade to weaken the foundations of the Christian faith.

To address the merits of Darwin's theory is beyond the scope of this book, and I will be happy to leave that to others. But I do recognize that ideas have consequences. And what Daniel C. Dennett has called "Darwin's Dangerous Idea"[19] has had huge and far-reaching consequences for mankind—now and in the future. (We have already seen that Darwin's concepts sent Karl Marx's thinking off in new and ultimately tragic directions.)

Contrary to what the title seems to suggest, the book *Darwin's Dangerous Idea* is actually a defense of Darwinism by a prominent evolutionary advocate. About the book, Nancy Pearcey has written:

The theory is "dangerous" only to irrational superstitions, like traditional religion and ethics, says the author Daniel Dennett. He calls

Darwinism a "universal acid," an allusion to the children's riddle about an acid so corrosive that it eats through everything—including the flask in which you are trying to contain it. The point is that Darwinism is likewise too corrosive to be contained. It spreads through every field of study, corroding away all traces of transcendent purpose or morality. As Dennett puts it, Darwinism "eats through just about every traditional concept and leaves in its wake a revolutionized world-view."[20]

On at least this one point, Dennett and I agree. Darwinism has eaten its way into every crevice of every nonbiblical worldview. As it has, it has indeed destroyed any sense that there are transcendent morals or absolute truths on which we can hang our hats or build meaningful lives. Once again, the end point of this line of thinking is postmodern nihilism. In other words, despair.

Today I walk among a generation of people who have been told by smug academic authorities that they are utterly insignificant and that their lives have no meaning. But as a student of the Bible, a preacher of the gospel, and a child of God, I have the privilege to refer them to a higher authority—one who declares, "You matter immensely, and your life is rich with meaning and eternal possibilities." And if you will excuse a relapse to my old unpolished eastern Kentucky vernacular for a moment, there is an old black book by my bedside that will still give you blessed assurance that you are somebody when everybody tries to tell you that, "You ain't nobody!" What a joy it is to relay that message.

SIGMUND FREUD

It's not very often that a researcher has the boldness to assert that he has created a whole new field of science—but that is essentially what Sigmund Freud claimed. This new branch of scientific inquiry was called psychology. And the world has never been the same.

Freud was born in 1856 in a part of Austria that now lies within the Czech Republic. Not much is known about Freud's early life, and that is apparently just the way he wanted it. On two occasions, in 1885 and 1907, Freud destroyed all of his personal papers and, with them, any written details of his personal life, thoughts, or actions. His secrecy continued beyond his death as his later papers were locked away in the Sigmund Freud Archives and were made available only to his handpicked biographer and a few trusted members of his inner circle of psychoanalysts.

What we do know a lot about are Freud's revolutionary ideas. Wikipedia encyclopedia summarized Freud's theories as the belief

> that human development is best understood in terms of changing objects of sexual desire; that the unconscious often represses wishes (generally of a sexual and aggressive nature); that unconscious conflicts over repressed wishes may express themselves in dreams and "Freudian slips"; that these unconscious conflicts are the source of neuroses; and that neurosis could be treated through bringing these unconscious wishes and repressed memories to consciousness in psychoanalytic treatment.[21]

In 1886, Freud opened a private practice in Vienna specializing in nervous and brain disorders. For a time he was a leading advocate of the use of cocaine for therapeutic purposes—until widespread reports of addiction created a backlash and forced him to retreat. He then began experimenting with hypnotism on his most hysterical patients but eventually abandoned the practice. In his forties, Freud became his own patient as he struggled with numerous psychosomatic disorders, a preoccupying fear of dying, and other phobias.

Freud and his theories became quite a sensation in European intellectual and social circles. Keep in mind that by the time Freud came onto the scene, Europe was nearly two hundred years into her reason-driven abandonment of biblical presuppositions.

Dave Breese described the popular appeal of Freud's theories in this way:

There broke upon the world the voice, the writings, and the mysterious perceptions of a man who seemed to have discovered how to define the nuances of the human psyche. Furthermore, his answers appeared to be not only scientific and scholarly, but interesting, provocative and even titillating.[22]

Like the other luminaries of the Age of Reason we have examined, Freud saw himself as a savior of mankind—a kind of messiah. One admiring biographer said Freud was a "leader determined to guide the human race towards the promised land."[27] And like the others, he felt it absolutely necessary to destroy the old foundation of biblical belief. Here are just two of the areas in which Freud's ideas clash with biblical revelation.

The Nature of Man—The Bible describes a three-part aspect to human existence. We see that man is spirit, soul, and body, with the soul composed of the mind, the will, and the emotions. My pastor, Dr. Lester Sumrall, brought the revelation of the threefold nature of man to the church, but unfortunately, many still misunderstand this biblical truth. Freud, like any good naturalist, completely rejected the possibility of the human spirit or of a spiritual dimension to the universe. But he did break human personality (the soul) down into three components—the *id*, the *ego*, and the *superego*. Nevertheless, according to Freud, man is still just a complex, highly evolved animal.

Faith—Freud viewed all religion and particularly Christian faith as a severe form of neurosis and generally childish. He once described the human tendency toward religion as "human infantilism" and "mass delusion."[24]

As with Darwin's theories, the concepts Freud introduced gave intellectuals a whole new set of impressive-sounding reasons to reject the Bible and its claims about Christ. As Dave Breese put it:

Freud, an atheist, gave every successive detractor of the value of religion a set of clever, psychological remarks through which to express contempt for God and His work.[25]

Like the theories of Karl Marx, most of Freud's ideas have now been thoroughly discredited by history and medical research. But, as with Marxism, that hasn't kept those ideas from continuing to influence the worldviews of many—including, as we'll see in a later chapter, many in the church.

Just how influential are these fathers of falsehood today? We'll see, as we now turn our attention to what is currently transpiring in the specific battleground areas of science, the arts, and the public square.

ACTION POINTS

- Support the rights of parents at the local, state and federal levels. Understand that the assumption that children ultimately belong to the government is rooted in the false and dangerous philosophy of Jean-Jacques Rousseau.
- Support proven "faith-based initiatives" to lift up the poor and oppressed as opposed to socialistic government measures built upon the discredited presuppositions of Karl Marx and his followers.
- Champion the inclusion of Intelligent Design research and thought in public discussions of the science of the universe's origins. Work to dispel the myth that all scientists are uniformly accepting of Darwin's theories.
- Counter the despair and hopelessness Darwinism produces in others by sharing with them the truth that God loves them, that they matter immensely, and that their lives are rich with meaning and eternal possibilities.
- Visit the C.S. Lewis Society's excellent Web site at www.apologetics.org for articles and resources on Marx, Freud, Darwin and other "Fathers of Falsehood."
- Suggested reading:

Seven Men Who Rule the World from the Grave, by Dave Breese[26]
Why Freud Was Wrong, by Richard Webster[27]

six

THE BATTLEGROUND OF SCIENCE

The 2005 movie *The Island* depicted a not-too-distant future in which wealthy individuals paid to have themselves cloned. In the film, the clone—referred to euphemistically as an "insurance policy"—was kept alive in isolated, ignorant bliss against some future day in which the clone's "owner" needed an organ transplant—at which point the clone would be killed and the needed organs "harvested."

In other words, conscious, feeling humans were being created in a laboratory purely for spare parts.

In spite of having a director with a string of blockbusters behind him and an A-list cast, the movie was uniformly trashed by the Hollywood critics. Perhaps they didn't like the uncomfortable light the movie shone on a couple of very current political issues—embryonic stem cell research and therapeutic cloning.

In truth, we are living in a day of almost unimaginable scientific possibilities. Yet as a moral culture, we have never been in a weaker position to manage those possibilities responsibly. As General Omar Bradley once put it, "We have grasped the mystery of the atom and rejected the Sermon on the Mount . . . The world has achieved brilliance without conscience. Ours is a world of nuclear giants and ethical infants."[1]

Does the plot of *The Island* seem far-fetched? Do you think

General Bradley's comment is overly dramatic? Think again. Below are just a few events and emerging technologies recently described in leading publications in this country:

- *Wired* magazine reported: "[Genetic researchers] postulate that . . . 350 key genes could be used to build the world's first artificial organism. Scientists could one day fashion customized organisms for eating radioactive waste, cleaning up oil spills, or generating renewable energy. Since the same genes could also be used to create biological superweapons, Venter and Fraser have temporarily postponed further experiments."[2]
- It was revealed in 1995 that an American biotechnology company had secretly made a cow-human hybrid embryo, by introducing the nucleus of a human cell into a cow egg. It lived for several days.[3]
- Chinese researchers have created part-human, part-rabbit embryos by inserting the nucleus from a young boy's cell into the hollowed-out egg of a rabbit. Intended to make embryos for stem cell research, the hybrids developed for several days in vitro. The researchers used rabbit cells because of the shortage of available human eggs.[4] Proponents of embryonic stem cell research fail to disclose the sheer numbers involved in their research. According to the Heritage Foundation, "To treat, for example, the 17 million diabetes patients in the United States will require a minimum of 850 million to 1.7 billion human eggs. Collecting 10 eggs per donor will require a minimum of 85 to 170 million women. The total cost would be astronomical . . ."[5]
- In 2002 a miniature pig was cloned that lacked both copies of a gene involved in immune rejection, raising the prospects of "xenotransplantation" of organs from pigs to humans.[6]
- Researchers in Tokyo have created an artificial plastic womb in which a fetus grows in amniotic fluid and is connected to machines through its umbilical cord. Designed to help women

with damaged or missing wombs, the artificial womb has already worked for goat fetuses and is projected to work for humans within a few years.[7]

- In an article titled "Mixing Species—and Crossing a Line?" a writer for *U.S. News & World Report* wrote about a stem-cell researcher who "began thinking about experiments in fetal mice that would replace part or all of their brains with human neural stem cells. A living mouse with a brain made entirely of human neurons could be a boon for scientists trying to test drugs aimed at the nervous system."[8]

- Researchers have speculated about the possibility of creating a human-chimpanzee hybrid—what some have called a "humanzee." Such a blending could theoretically create a cheap labor force of reasonably intelligent workers with amazing strength that could be deployed to do menial and dirty tasks.[9]

We must face the disturbing fact that technology is racing forward so quickly, policy makers and so-called bioethicists can't possibly keep up. And even when a highly questionable line of research *is* banned in the United States, it usually continues unregulated in places like China and South Korea.

To his credit, President George W. Bush tried to call attention to this problem and rally consensus in his 2006 State of the Union speech when he said:

Tonight I ask you to pass legislation to prohibit the most egregious abuses of medical research: human cloning in all its forms, creating or implanting embryos for experiments, creating human-animal hybrids, and buying, selling, or patenting human embryos. Human life is a gift from our Creator—and that gift should never be discarded, devalued or put up for sale.

Let that sink in for a moment. *We are living in a day in which a U.S. president felt it necessary to call for legislation banning the creation of human-animal hybrids.* Human cloning and the development of human-animal hybrids sounds unthinkable. But I was privileged to be one of a small group who was invited to the White House to witness President Bush veto a bill that would overturn the limits on federal funding for embryonic stem cell research. The future has arrived, and we are unprepared for it.

Now, overlay that with what I pointed out in Chapter 1—the growing presence of a militant group of scientists and academics like Richard Dawkins and Peter Singer who have moved from merely defending their scientific views against critiques from creationists, to aggressively attacking Christianity and Bible-based moral principles.

Put the two trends together and a chilling picture emerges. At the very moment science in our civilization most desperately needs the light of biblical wisdom, it is aggressively moving to extinguish all traces of that light.

FAITH VS. SCIENCE?

The current adversarial climate has made many Christians think they must choose between science and faith. It has also convinced many decent men and women in the scientific community that they must reject all religious influence in order to be faithful to science.

But this is a false dilemma. The fact is, science, properly understood, is a natural extension of Christian faith. As Baylor University professor Rodney Stark convincingly argues in his book *For the Glory of God: How Monotheism Led to Reformations, Science, Witch-Hunts, and the End of Slavery*, modern science owes its very existence to the emergence of biblical Christianity in Europe!

> [T]he rise of science was not an extension of classical learning. It was the natural outgrowth of Christian doctrine: Nature exists because it was created by God. To love and honor God, one must fully appreci-

ate the wonders of His handiwork. Moreover, because God is perfect, His handiwork functions in accordance with *immutable principles* . . . These were crucial ideas, and that's why the rise of science occurred in Christian Europe, not somewhere else.[10]

Nevertheless, even modest recent attempts by proponents of intelligent design to break the Darwinists' monopoly in school curricula have been met with vehement opposition and triggered well-funded, well-organized attacks.

For example, in 2005, when the nine-member Dover Pennsylvania School Board backed a requirement that biology students at least be exposed to the intelligent design position in order to compare it to the Darwinist position already extensively taught, they were buried in a national avalanche of media-fueled scorn and criticism.

Represented by lawyers for the ACLU and cheered on by the group Americans United for the Separation of Church and State, some parents took the school district to court. At the same time, a slate of anti–intelligent design candidates was recruited to challenge eight of the members who were up for reelection. With a war chest from a nationwide fund-raising effort, astonishing levels of political organization for a simple school board race, and wall-to-wall friendly media coverage—all eight of the sitting school board members were swept out of office.

Please don't ever think that local elections are inconsequential. They matter a great deal and are often the easiest to impact. It is easy to see how a church satisfied with sitting on padded pews under crystal chandeliers cannot impact a community in the way Christ intended when He clearly told us to be salt and light in our culture. When the church retreats into her religious enclaves and allows the world to go on its wayward course undeterred, the culture is directed by those with a point of view antithetical to the Bible. These viewpoints cannot help but prevail if those who say they uphold morality abandon the field.

When the case finally went to court, Judge John E. Jones III issued a scathing ruling striking down the Dover School District's policy and sharply criticizing the former school board members. Of the decision, Jan LaRue, chief counsel for Concerned Women of America, wrote: "It strains credulity to imagine how a statement devoid of religious reference establishes religion. [Judge] Jones had no reason to decide whether Intelligent Design is good or bad scientific theory in order to answer the narrow question of whether the school district officials acted from improper religious motivation. It's a classic example of judicial activism when a judge does that."[11]

In my book *Silent No More*, I devoted an entire chapter to this issue of judicial activism, titling that section "Judicial Tyranny." Although as I point out in the book, the problem is huge, entrenched, and institutionalized, there is cause to be hopeful. At that time I wrote: "The trends of the last decades can be changed. We can reclaim the nation our fathers envisioned. We can start a grassroots movement that induces our elected leaders to assert themselves over the courts."[12] "Clearly, we have moved away from the literal meaning of the law and moved to what scholars call 'legal realism' or 'sociological jurisprudence.' This means simply that the law is whatever the judges say it is, because the judges are no longer bound by the literal meaning of the law."[13]

I am more hopeful now than ever. Since the publication of *Silent No More*, we have seen the addition of not one, but two United States Supreme Court justices who hold great promise for restoring the role of the courts to the limited place intended by the Founding Fathers. These court appointments are a vivid demonstration of why elections matter. And why it is so important that God's people be informed, be heard, and be counted.

As I write, our state and national legislators confront a host of complex policy questions regarding science and medicine. These are life-and-death questions in which wisdom and moral clarity are desperately needed. You need to know about them. And your representatives need to hear what you know. Let's explore some of the most pressing.

FLASH POINTS ON THE
BATTLEGROUND OF SCIENCE

EMBRYONIC STEM CELL RESEARCH

He was a brilliant choice of spokesman for the cause of embryonic stem cell research (ESCR). Christopher Reeve, who had been a popular and accomplished actor before being completely paralyzed in a horseback riding accident in 1995, was universally admired for the courage and determination he showed following the accident. That's why it was so difficult for many to respond vigorously and appropriately when Reeve sat in his wheelchair before a congressional committee in April of 2000 and encouraged aggressive federal funding of ESCR. Few wanted to have to point out that much of what Reeve told the assembled legislators and nationwide news audience was simply wrong or misleading.

At the heart of the ongoing controversy is a special type of cell called a stem cell. In 1998, researchers using tissue from aborted babies discovered that an embryo's early cells, or stem cells, under the right conditions, could turn into any type of human tissue.

In what almost seemed like some sort of magic trick, these stem cells could be programmed to develop into muscle, neurons, fat, heart tissue, or skin. At first blush, the applications of this discovery seemed breathtaking. If doctors could harness enough stem cells, and transplant them into damaged heart tissue, for example, the stem cells could be stimulated to form new heart muscle, and the damage would slowly disappear.

The problem, of course, was that human embryos had to be destroyed, and in large numbers, if an adequate number of stem cells were going to be harvested. As White House Fellow Richard Greco Jr. has pointed out:

> [I]t became clear that great multitudes of embryos would be necessary to provide enough stem cells for treatment. Estimates using data from the National Academy of Sciences, the National Research

Council, and the University of Wisconsin, show that to treat just 10 percent of all potential patients, 13.4 million genetically thatched human embryos would have to be created and destroyed. To give you some perspective, that is one-and-a-half times the current population of New York City.[14]

Of course, for defenders of unlimited abortion on demand and others who have convinced themselves that a developing baby in the womb is not human—nothing more than fetal tissue—this poses no ethical problems whatsoever. "We can and should produce and destroy as many human embryos as needed, especially if living adults and children might experience remarkable cures as a result," they reason.

However, not all of us have bought in to the unborn-humans-aren't-"persons" line of thinking. We know our history too well.

We know that this was precisely the rationale that was used to defend slavery for centuries; and that it was central to the infamous *Dred Scott* decision by the U.S. Supreme Court that upheld slavery as an institution in America until the Civil War and Lincoln's Emancipation Proclamation brought it to an end. And we remember that it was used by the Nazis to justify and rationalize the murder of six million of Europe's Jews.

Thus, the national debate over ESCR has become entwined with our ongoing cultural and political divisions over the abortion question.

What proponents of ESCR are slow to acknowledge is the growing body of research which shows that there are other viable, more effective sources of stem cells—adult stem cells; umbilical cord blood; and placental tissue. None of these sources of stem cells requires destroying a developing human being in order to acquire them. I like the way Chuck Colson put it: "We don't have to kill one person to cure another. The three remaining sources of stem cells present no ethical problems whatsoever."[15]

Nevertheless, Ron Reagan, son of former President Ronald Reagan, was handed a prime-time speaking slot at the Democratic

National Convention in 2004 so he could perpetuate one of the biggest myths about this complex issue.

It has been incessantly charged that the Bush administration has "banned stem cell research." This is the big lie that has been repeated so often and with such conviction, few people actually know that it's not true. As I mentioned in my book *Silent No More*, ". . . we let myths that are repeated often enough take on the assumed authority of fact."[16] In reality, President Bush rightly placed restrictions on *federal funding* of *embryonic* stem cell research. His executive order leaves state governments and private companies free to pursue whatever type of research they choose. And federal funds remain available for *adult* stem cell research—the most medically promising area of all!

All the president did was to keep you and me from having our tax dollars appropriated for the destruction of thousands of viable human embryos.

During an interview on a prime time national news program, the interviewer indicated to me that researchers maintained that embryonic stem cell research held "great promise." But what researcher worth his Ph.D. would attempt to attract funding for a line of research that he said had no promise?

Private foundations and research organizations are providing some funding for embryonic stem cell research, but they are counting on far greater contributions from the public sector. Since the federal government has limited these funds, researchers are turning to the states, and in some cases, most notably New Jersey, California, and Connecticut, they are finding more and more support for using tax revenues to finance what amounts to the destruction of human lives.

THERAPEUTIC CLONING

Two years after his initial and sadly inaccurate testimony before Congress, Christopher Reeve was back. In March of 2002, Reeve—the handpicked spokesman for an elite group of research activists—repeated his plea for ESCR but added a new angle. He called for federal support and endorsement of therapeutic cloning—the practice of creating a cloned embryo of a person in order to "harvest" stem cells that perfectly match the patient's own DNA.

He argued that spinal cord injury cases like his own might be cured only if such cloning were legal and supported.

You can now see why so many on the "progressive" Left Coast in the country resented *The Island,* the movie I mentioned at the opening of this chapter. What advocates of therapeutic cloning (like the late Christopher Reeve) propose is not all that different from the frightening premise of the movie. The only difference is that, for the time being anyway, the "harvesting" of the needed material is done at the embryonic stage of human development. But will it end there? If history is a guide, it will not.

That is why the president's 2006 State of the Union address calling for a ban on all forms of cloning, including therapeutic cloning, was so timely. That a president of the United States would mention this issue in such an important speech indicates the seriousness of the moral, ethical, and spiritual crisis we now face. There are many, even in positions of authority, who would think nothing of cloning a human embryo and then destroying it in the name of research.

Here in my home state of Ohio, the Center for Moral Clarity helped marshal grassroots support for a Human Cloning Prohibition Act in 2005. Unfortunately, the bill never made it out of committee in either the House of Representatives or the Senate, but we will not stop advocating these kinds of restrictions. In a similar way, people of conscience everywhere must make themselves heard . . . before it is too late. Our way of life is threatened, not only by terrorists who would turn back the clock, denying centuries of progress, but by scientists and marketers who would thrust us forward into a future where human life becomes nothing more than a commodity, like stocks or currency. We were critical of our government because they failed to see a threat materializing before the terrorist attacks of 9-11. What will history say about those who sit idly by and deny the threat that cloning poses to the future of humanity?

SEX-SELECTION AND HEALTH-SELECTION ABORTIONS

All around the world, births of girl babies tend to slightly outnumber births of boys. Worldwide, about 1,050 girls are born for every 1,000 boys. But not in the Punjab province of India. There, only 600 girls are born for every 1,000 boys.[17]

What is causing this huge discrepancy? A practice called female feticide—the aborting of a baby as soon as it is discovered that she is a girl. According to a recent article in the British newspaper *The Daily Telegraph*, this practice is "so widespread in India because of the preference for sons rather than daughters that *The Lancet* recently estimated that 10 million baby girls had been terminated in the past 20 years."[18]

As I hear about these developments, I can't help but wonder where radical feminism is in this matter. Why is their voice so obviously missing from those that are raised against this practice? Aren't they concerned about the rights of all women everywhere? Perhaps their silence on this issue is because feminism is more interested in a woman's right to have an abortion than it is with an unborn woman's right to live.

Not surprisingly, after decades of this practice, there is a severe shortage of brides in Punjab province. According to the article, "Men in their twenties are unable to find wives because more than a quarter of the normal female population is missing."[19] China is facing a similar shortage of brides for the same reasons.

Of course, those are strange, faraway places. Such a practice could never flourish here in the United States, could it? Yes, it could. In fact, it's a growing trend.

No, our culture doesn't have a widespread preference for boys. But when it comes to their future child's sex, many parents do have a strong preference one way or the other. Now, a new type of home test kit enables pregnant women to know whether they're having a boy or a girl, almost as soon as they know they're expecting. A *Boston Globe* article about the new tests pointed out the obvious implications of them:

Just two or three days after mailing the test overnight to a Lowell lab for processing, a pregnant woman can know what color to paint the nursery—or even decide whether to get an abortion if she wants a child of the opposite sex, a prospect that worries ethicists.[20]

My view is that it ought to do more than worry ethicists. It ought to worry all of us. In fact, it ought to do more than worry us, it ought to infuriate us all. Do we really have our heads so far in the sand that we cannot see the consequences of these actions? The fact is, any society that can convince itself that something as horrific and unnecessary as partial birth abortion is a vital right will have very few qualms about women aborting their babies because they happen to be the wrong sex.

Such a people will have even fewer reservations about aborting children who are by their own personal and subjective standards less than perfect. Sadly, that too is on the rise.

Everyone wants a perfect baby. But a growing segment of Americans feel they have a right to one. And increasingly sophisticated medical technology is making the exercise of that "right" easier all the time.

As a recent *New York Times* article reported:

"Fetal genetic tests are now routinely used to diagnose diseases as well known as cystic fibrosis and as obscure as fragile X, a form of mental retardation. High-resolution sonograms can detect life-threatening defects like brain cysts as well as treatable conditions like a small hole in the heart or a cleft palate sooner and more reliably than previous generations of the technology. And the risk of Down syndrome, one of the most common birth defects, can be assessed in the first trimester rather than waiting for a second-trimester blood test or amniocentesis."[21]

I don't for one moment wish to trivialize the heartbreak and soul-wrenching anguish parents feel when they learn that the precious life they have anticipated and dreamed about is less than whole and will have a difficult, possibly abbreviated life.

You don't pastor a congregation of thousands, as I have done for thirty years, without having put your arms around scores of devastated couples who have received bad news—praying for them, quietly encouraging them, weeping with them. All the while knowing that at that dark moment no words could possibly diminish the sting of disappointment they feel, or provide a satisfying answer to the cry of their questioning hearts.

My amazing wife, Joni, and I have drunk from that cup of disappointment and wrestled with those questions. As she shared in the Epilogue to *Silent No More*, we lost our desperately desired and very eagerly anticipated daughter, Abigail, before she ever saw a sunrise. As Joni wrote so transparently: "The devastation that I felt over the loss of this little life was suffocating—every breath seemed a conscious effort. My once tranquil soul became a tidal wave of emotion as grief washed over every ounce of my being."[22]

As I watch our daughter, Ashton, now seventeen, enjoying her senior year of high school, I'm reminded of facing an astounding choice given to Joni and me by those in the medical community. Early in Joni's pregnancy with Ashton, she was given the standard AFP (Alphafoetoprotein) test which determines the possibility of certain abnormalities.

Joni and I were called and told to come in right away to our obstetrician's office because the levels were very low. We were given a list of possibilities as a result: Down syndrome, Spina Bifida, Fragile X, and even death.

Our next step was a series of intensive ultrasounds where measurements and other studies could be done to determine any pre-existing signs of the aforementioned defects. After the second Level II ultrasound, my wife asked what was the reason for all of this if nothing could be done to help the baby in utero. The radiologist quickly responded, "So you have enough time, given the results, to terminate the pregnancy".

Joni rose up and emphatically stated, "I don't believe in abortion, and we want this baby no matter what." After consulting with our doctor, we ceased any further testing. He explained the fallibility of the AFP test (given to all pregnant women) because there are many variables that determine its accuracy. Imagine how many women and couples may have aborted their child just on the notion that something might be wrong. What if we had given in to that fear?

Our daughter was born a healthy 9 pounds 1 ounce, and in 14 years of school has never made a B. She maintains a 4.32 GPA, is a cheerleader, class president, 3-sport athlete, has been the recipient of many honors and is distinguished not only at her school, but also locally and nationally.

I only say that to show that those low AFP levels did not affect her intelligence or her health. Thank God, we chose to believe Him and in His report, for beyond her many recognitions, what makes Ashton special is simply that she is Ashton—a unique design of God and His wonderful handiwork. We valued Ashton's life before she ever won an award or a prestigious honor because we valued her life before she was born.

Technology, left unguided by moral discipline, is our present-day "Tower of Babel", and it is providing us with choices that feed the almighty god of "self". When did a life, seen as imperfect, become so disposable? Had Ashton been born with any of these abnormalities, she would still be as precious to us and as valuable to the fabric of our family, as well as society. What and where would our society be without the countless contributions made and inspired by those with special needs or handicaps of any sort? Let us ever keep before us the admonition of Job 12:10: "In His hand is the life of every creature and the breath of all mankind."

So please don't think we take this stand for life callously or without compassion. But stand for life we must. You see, our nation is rushing headlong toward a future in which few of us are going to want to live. One in which many are denied the right to live—simply because they are "imperfect", inconvenient, or for that matter, merely female.

Right on America's northern border, nurses in many hospitals are now forced to assist in late-term abortions of handicapped babies.[23] Here in America, there are many anecdotal reports of parents actually being pressured to abort pregnancies once Down syndrome has been diagnosed.

Stephen Nelson, staff neonatologist and director of the Neonatal Transport Service at MeritCare Children's Hospital in Fargo, North Dakota, told *Christianity Today:* "There's a lot of unspoken pressure to abort once you've had the testing done. Throughout the medical literature, parents are blamed if they have a baby with Down syndrome. Parents who decide to give birth to a Down syndrome child say that they feel like outcasts."[24]

Consider this. According to a March 22, 2006, news story by Reuters:

North Korea has no people with physical disabilities because they are killed almost as soon as they are born, a physician who defected from the communist state said on Wednesday.

Ri Kwang-chol, who fled to the South last year, told a forum of rights activists that the practice of killing newborns was widespread but denied he himself took part in it.

He said babies born with physical disabilities were killed in infancy in hospitals or in homes and were quickly buried.

The practice is encouraged by the state, Ri said, as a way of purifying the masses and eliminating people who might be considered "different."[25]

Is this a glimpse of our future? It is unless you and I raise our voices against the perverse, upside-down deception that encourages the deaths of innocents and looks with condemnation and disdain on those who choose unselfish love and life-giving grace. At the continuing risk of being misunderstood, misquoted and maligned, I will continue to stridently and strenuously object to all who advocate such heinous practices. But I will object just as strongly to all who choose to sit by and let outrages such as these go unnoticed, unchallenged, and unrestrained.

REENGINEERING HUMANITY

As I write, two areas of science are converging to hold out a tantalizing promise to the next generations of humans on planet earth—superhuman abilities and astonishing life spans.

Is this overstating the case? Not if you read any of the future-oriented literature coming out these days. Look, for example, at this breathless excerpt from a 1997 issue of the technology magazine *Wired*:

> During the past five years a slow collision of epic proportions has united two disparate fields of science. The slow collision is between computer science and human biology. The result promises to be an explosion of new knowledge and power that will sever us from our human heritage and transform us in ways that we cannot yet imagine . . . Once the full sequence of human DNA has been disassembled and annotated, we will be able to recompile the resulting code for our own purposes. We will customize ourselves and our children—and, by extension, their children and their children's children. In this way, we will change the course of evolution itself.[26]

Since that article was written, the "full sequence of human DNA" has indeed been completely annotated. The Human Genome Project was completed in April of 2003. Now some say we are standing on the threshold of a "brave new world" in which we customize our children the way we currently pick the color and options on a new car; extend healthy life spans to 120 years, 150 years, or longer; and begin the process of becoming "trans-human," as we increasingly merge our biological selves with robotic devices and computers through nanotechnology.

As Nigel Cameron of the Center for Bioethics and Human Dignity said recently: "Abortion and euthanasia are *taking* life, cloning is *making* life, and nanotechnology and cybernetics are *faking* life. Nanotechnology . . . holds the dangerous potential of controlling or possibly even re-engineering human nature."[27]

All this may indeed be technologically possible in a very short time. But just because it *can* be done, doesn't mean it *should* be done.

I am convinced that the only hope we have of wisely managing mankind's emerging technological power is through a sweeping, culture-wide move toward God in humility and reverence. There was a time-honored word for such a move where I grew up. *Revival.*

In the second half of this book, I'll lay out a plan for bringing just such a move of God to our shores. But before I do, we have two additional battlegrounds to scout out.

ACTION POINTS

- Refuse to accept the lie that you must choose between faith and science.
- Become involved in school board elections and support candidates who understand the value of exposing science students to working origins theories like Intelligent Design.
- Let your representatives know that you oppose state or federal funding of embryonic stem cell research and other forms of research that require the destruction of human embryos.
- Speak out against the growing trend toward sex selection abortions and the aborting of babies with mild birth defects. Point out the slippery slope on which such killing places our society.
- Support organizations like The Center for Bioethics and Human Dignity, The Family Research Council, and The Center for Moral Clarity that are working to bring wider understanding to complex issues like embryonic stem cell research.
- Visit www.cbhd.com, the information-rich Web site by the Center for Bioethics and Human Dignity and acquaint yourself with the key issues and the latest legislative battles.
- Suggested reading:

For the Glory of God: How Monotheism Led to Reformations, Science, Witch-Hunts, and the End of Slavery, by Rodney Stark.[28]

Life, Liberty, and the Defense of Dignity: The Challenge for Bioethics, by Leon R. Kass, M.D.[29]

Our Posthuman Future: Consequences of the Biotechnology Revolution, by Francis Fukuyama.[30]

seven

THE BATTLEGROUND OF THE ARTS

Throughout 2005 and early 2006, worldwide controversy escalated over the publication in Europe of political cartoons that depicted Islam's founder, Mohammed. Most of the cartoons were making points about the increasing identification of radical Islamists with terrorism. A small group of Danish cartoonists had actually created the cartoons as a test of Europe's commitment to freedom of expression and freedom of the press in the face of what they saw as the growing "Islamification" of Europe.

The results of that test were indeed enlightening.

A group of Islamic clerics assembled those published cartoons (throwing in some unpublished ones that were much more inflammatory for added effect) and took them around the capitals of the Islamic world for the express purpose of generating outrage. And outrage they got.

As you probably know, street riots and embassy burnings ensued in Iran, Pakistan, Libya, and elsewhere in the Middle East, with loss of life occurring in several places. In Nigeria alone, fifteen people died in riot-related violence.

Initially, the cartoons were a political statement expressed on the editorial pages of a few newspapers. But once the widespread riots and deaths over the cartoons began, it became a major *news* story. As a result, numerous newspapers in Europe reprinted the cartoons in news stories to show what all the fuss was about. In their view, journalistic integrity and consistency demanded it.

Why mention this set of events in a book about the culture wars in America? Because one particular set of reactions by a major media institution here in the United States perfectly captures the current cultural climate and the nature of the battle we're facing.

You see, like their European counterparts, U.S. news organizations were faced with a journalistic dilemma. The Muslim riots and deaths made the cartoons a legitimate news story. So many observers wondered which, if any, U.S. newspapers would reprint the cartoons in connection with their coverage. In particular, all eyes were on the *New York Times,* the pre-eminent newspaper in the nation.

On February 6, 2006, the *Times* gave us its decision in an editorial:

> [We] and much of the rest of the nation's news media have reported on the cartoons but refrained from showing them. That seems a reasonable choice **for news organizations that usually refrain from gratuitous assaults on religious symbols**, especially since the cartoons are so easy to describe in words. (emphasis added)

Fair enough, you may think. But wait . . . there's more!

On the following day . . . I repeat . . . the very next day, the Arts section of the *Times* ran a photograph of a work of "art" by British artist Chris Ofili titled "Holy Virgin Mary." It was essentially a photographic collage depicting the Virgin Mary composed of elephant dung and overlaid with cut-out sections of images from pornographic magazines. (You'll notice that I didn't have to show you this piece of filth. It was, in the words of the *Times,* "easy to describe in words.") Nevertheless, the image was printed.

Aren't you glad the *Times* editors have such strong convictions about refraining "from gratuitous assaults on religious symbols"? The editors at the *New York Times* happily printed an image that was surely deeply offensive to the world's one billion Roman Catholics and the vast majority of the one billion non-Catholic Christians around the world. Sadly, it probably never even occurred to the editors not to run it.

To add to the breathtaking hypocrisy of the incident, Michael Kimmelman, the author of the article that featured the "Holy Virgin Mary" photograph, is on record as calling the Danish cartoons "callous and feeble."[1]

What I want you to see is, in the increasingly overlapping worlds of art, entertainment, and media news, double standards and hypocrisy abound—particularly when it comes to discussing and portraying traditional Christianity.

In the battle for the hearts and minds of the current generation of Americans, this is where the stakes are highest and the weapons are most powerful. As a result, in the war of ideas, these are areas where the conflict is most intense.

Let's briefly visit each area as we identify a few of the most serious challenges as well as some causes for hope and encouragement.

FILM AND TELEVISION:
"JIMMY STEWART, WE MISS YOU"

World War II brought some days of stern testing to our nation. America and her allies faced powerful, determined enemies and had to fight a war, not on two fronts, but in two separate "theaters" on opposite sides of the planet. It was a time of remarkable sacrifice, cohesiveness, and unity in our country. And with very few exceptions, the men and women of Hollywood stepped up and did their part.

For example, some of the biggest stars of the time put their careers aside and enlisted for military service. Jimmy Stewart, arguably Hollywood's top male actor, joined the Army Air Corps and, as a squadron commander, led twenty separate B-24 bombing raids over Germany. He ultimately earned the rank of colonel, as well as the Air Medal, the Distinguished Flying Cross, the Croix de Guerre, and seven battle stars. After the war, Stewart continued in the U.S. Air Force Reserve and became a brigadier general.

Other leading men, including such well known stars as Douglas Fairbanks, Jr. and Gene Autry, as well as lesser lights such as James Arness, Eddie Albert, and Walter Matthau, also enlisted and served with distinction.

John Wayne tried three different times to enlist—first in the army, then in the navy, then in director John Ford's photographic unit. But Wayne had been classified 4-F due to an ongoing back problem and was rejected each time. Frustrated, he applied what he did best in support of the cause. He joined a vast array of other Hollywood actors, writers, and directors, who churned out movies designed to boost the country's morale and steel our national will to fight.

Hollywood's women were not to be outdone. Most, like Bette Davis, Judy Garland, Paulette Goddard, and Ann Sheridan, found creative ways to support the troops—through films, USO shows, and fund-raising for war bonds.

Consider the Austrian-born actress Hedy Lamarr—a remarkable combination of beauty, brains, and fighting spirit. In addition to making significant technical contributions to a new type of radio-controlled torpedo for Allied use, Lamarr single-handedly raised more than $7 million in bonds for the war effort. She did this mostly by selling kisses at rallies and USO events across America.

To put Lamarr's efforts in perspective and in inflation-adjusted terms, that would be like Gwyneth Paltrow going around today and personally raising more than $80 million to support the troops in Iraq and Afghanistan. Which, by the way, is not likely to happen. Following the 9-11 attacks on America, Paltrow—who was expecting her first child—announced to the British press that she planned to stay in England rather than move back to her native America. Apparently, she found all the post-attack flag waving and patriotism a little creepy. "I worry about bringing up a child in America," Paltrow told reporters. "At the moment, there's a weird, over-patriotic atmosphere over there."[2] It's interesting to me that Americans once referred to Europe as "over there"—in fact, that was the title of a popular song during World War I.

Someone should let Ms. Paltrow know that she can come on back home now. Flag waving has definitely fallen out of fashion. "God Bless America" is out. Bashing the commander in chief and criticizing the troops are in—especially in Hollywood.

Not so in 1943. During that year's Academy Awards ceremony, actors Alan Ladd and Tyrone Power stood on the stage and held up a banner honoring Hollywood's servicemen and women. Fast-forward six decades to the 2003 Oscar ceremony. There we find Michael Moore being honored by the Academy for his antigun documentary, *Bowling for Columbine*—the predecessor to his grotesquely dishonest Bush-bashing documentary, *Fahrenheit 911*. We also find Moore using his allotted forty-five seconds of acceptance speech time to question the legitimacy of Bush's election and to shout, "We are against this war! Shame on you, Mr. Bush! Shame on you!" Some of the assembled actors stood up and cheered, while some of the regular folks up in the cheap seats booed.

Clearly, the days of broad-based Hollywood support for a strong, free America are long gone. In its place, there seems to be a pervasive hatred of American patriotism, traditional morality, and above all, biblical Christianity.

I could fill five hundred pages with outrageous quotes by celebrities and entertainment industry luminaries. You would hear from all the usual suspects: Barbra Streisand, George Clooney, Woody Harrelson, Meryl Streep, Tim Robbins, Susan Sarandon, Alec Baldwin—on and on the roster would run. And most of those would betray the deeply held humanist, Marxist, or nihilist worldviews so pervasive in the entertainment industry.

As David Limbaugh points out in his excellent book *Persecution: How Liberals Are Waging War Against Christianity*:

In the documented bias against Christians and Christianity in our modern culture, Hollywood and Big Media play very major roles . . .

both of these major cultural power centers routinely disparage Christians and present them in a negative light. This anti-Christian bias manifests itself in unflattering portrayals of Christians in Hollywood films and entertainment television and also in the demonization of Christian conservatives in the media.[3]

At the same time the elites of pop culture will go to extreme lengths to avoid offending other groups—particularly, as we saw with the *New York Times,* Muslims.

I remember how pleased I was to hear that Tom Clancy's excellent novel *The Sum of All Fears* was going to be made into a movie. In the novel, a CIA agent tries to thwart a group of Islamic extremists who gain control of a nuclear warhead and plot to detonate it at the Super Bowl. Written well before the September 11 attacks on our nation, the novel now seems eerily accurate in its presentation of a terrorist attack. But if you saw the movie, you know that the screenwriters replaced the Muslim militants with a neo-Nazi group! (Of course, the views of neo-Nazis and white supremacists are demonic and abhorrent, but did their substitution in the movie plot make it more or less credible? Why make that change?)

The fact is, neo-Nazis and Christians, along with the invariably evil "multinational corporation," are now Hollywood's three remaining "safe," all-purpose bad guys for movie plots. And many movie and television scripts tend to make Christians and neo-Nazis out to be pretty much the same thing.

Christian leaders, including myself, with few exceptions condemned the horror of the Oklahoma City bombing, masterminded by Timothy McVeigh. However, there are comparatively few voices from the Muslim world that similarly condemn the atrocities of the radical Islamic extremists who are determined to use terrorism as their weapon of choice in their attempt to overthrow Christian civilization.

Another key cultural issue of our time involves the very definition of marriage and family. Of course, Hollywood is doing its part to try to "normalize" homosexual marriage, gay adoption, and "alternative" forms of family composition. One of the most bold of these is HBO's series *Big Love,* which follows the trials and stresses of a polygamist man with three wives. Conservative social observers like Stanley Kurtz have been warning us for some time that the gay marriage movement was just the tip of the spear. He has predicted that the same arguments currently being put forth in advocacy of gay marriage will quickly be followed by moves to legitimize polygamy and polyamory (multiple individuals all being "married" to each other).[4]

With *Big Love,* some in Hollywood are already working to soften up opposition to those efforts.

Clearly, the entertainment industry is one of the most hostile and alien places a Christian in America could possibly work. But that is precisely why it is so exciting to see a small but growing vanguard of committed believers doing just that. Instead of abandoning these arts to the enemies of faith and traditional values, these committed actors, writers, and producers are excelling within it. They are following the Biblical injunction to be in the world, even though they are not of the world.

And since the huge successes of *The Passion of the Christ* and *The Chronicles of Narnia*, this encouraging trend is growing. So much so, that it is now on the radar of the mainstream press. In a recent article in *The Atlantic* magazine titled "Can Jesus Save Hollywood?" writer Hanna Rosin points to the rising profile of authentic Christians in Hollywood and to organizations like Act One, a Los Angeles–based support network and training program for aspiring Christian screenwriters.[5]

In the article "Salting Hollywood," *World Magazine* highlighted the "Hollywood Prayer Network—which consists of some 3,500 Christians in the industry who pray for each other and for their non-Christian colleagues" and profiled Ralph Winters, a born-again producer behind several successful films.

And listeners of NPR's *Morning Edition* heard an upcoming segment introduced this way:

Monique Parsons reports on Christians and Hollywood—two words that don't normally appear together. But Parsons finds that many in Tinseltown use their faith to shape, and interpret, the movies and films they work on.[6]

The same is true in other areas of the entertainment and media world. Look closely into the worlds of popular music, journalism, broadcasting, and literature, and you will find talented, hardworking believers there being salt and light—and doing great work. They are Daniels in a Babylonian court and, like Daniel, exerting influence and redeeming all they handle. But as we'll see, there is much that needs their touch.

ART, ARCHITECTURE, AND MUSIC: PERVERSE NONSENSE

The opening lines of the Bible present God to us as a Creator, and therefore as possessing infinite creativity. And because the Bible also declares that man is made in God's image and likeness, it is my belief that the same divine spark of creativity lies within us as well.

In all times and in all places, humans have felt compelled to express that spark through art, music, story, and architecture. But it was in a Europe fully immersed in a Christian worldview that these forms reached their highest levels. In the Renaissance, we find all of these disciplines being deployed to glorify God and to point people to Him.

Classical music may not be your cup of tea, but I challenge you to listen to a Bach concerto without marveling at the order and beautiful intricacy of the work. The soaring Gothic cathedrals of Europe may now be empty and devoid of spiritual life, but they still stand majestically after a thousand years. How many of our modern church buildings will still be here even one hundred years from now?

In the paintings and scientific sketches of Da Vinci, in the art of Michelangelo, and in the works of scores of other Renaissance artists you'll find two things—a commitment to *beauty* and a belief in *order*. The first stems from the Bible-based assumption that the Creator is glorious and that everything He made, prior to the fall, was beautiful as well. The second was a direct outgrowth of the presupposition that God had created the universe orderly and predictable.

Of course, not every artist—then or now—who creates something beautiful is a full-fledged Christian. As Francis Schaeffer observed:

> It is not only Christians who can paint with beauty, nor for that matter only Christians who can love or who have creative stirrings. Even though the image is now contorted, people are made in the image of God. This is who people are, whether or not they know or acknowledge it. God is the great Creator, and part of the unique mannishness of man, as made in God's image, is creativity.[7]

True enough. However, as I pointed out in a previous chapter, as Western civilization began to reject the biblical worldview, that abandonment gradually began to be reflected in the arts. Beginning about one hundred years ago, art, music, and eventually even architecture began to move away from the twin ideals of beauty and order.

It's no surprise then that, for many, the very term *modern art* has become a synonym for perversity or nonsense—or frequently, *perverse nonsense*. It was the cartoonist Al Capp who defined abstract art as "a product of the untalented, sold by the unprincipled to the utterly bewildered."[8]

I won't defile your imagination by even describing what passes for good art in the trendy galleries of New York, Los Angeles, London, and Paris these days. Besides, you've heard the horror stories and outrages many times—from Robert Mapplethorpe's quasi-pornographic photographs to Damien Hirst's repeated use of dead sheep in jars of formaldehyde to what Andres Serrano felt compelled to submerge a crucifix in—all is praised as cutting-edge art. The uglier and more chaotic, the better, seems to be the rule.

It's enough to make Michelangelo's statue *David* weep real tears.

Classical music also began to purposefully move away from beauty and order. A new breed of composers in the early twentieth century began to carry Darwinist and materialist assumptions to their logical musical conclusions. Aaron Copland, John Cage, Arnold Schoenberg, and many others began experimenting with new forms that abandoned traditional constraints of rhythm, meter, key, and melody. More "progressive" composers produced works that sound like the musical corollary to Jackson Pollock's random slinging of paint at a canvas.

This trend ultimately migrated over to the pop music side in the form of punk, death metal, and other nihilistic styles that exalt disorder, darkness, and decay.

No area of creativity or design seems to have been immune from these forces. For example, in my hometown of Columbus, Ohio, you'll find a bizarre-looking building called the Wexner Center for the Arts, named for a well-known entrepreneur who built a veritable empire of nationally known retail chains and is a benefactor to the city. The wonderful Christian apologist Ravi Zacharias mentioned this piece of modern architecture in a 2002 address to the United Nations' Prayer Breakfast. Zacharias told his audience:

> I remember lecturing at Ohio State University. I was minutes away from beginning my lecture, and my host was driving me past a new building called the Wexner Center for the Performing Arts. He said, "This is America's first postmodern building."
>
> I was startled for a moment and I said, "What is a postmodern building?" He said, "Well, the architect said that he designed this building with no design in mind. When the architect was asked, 'Why?' he said, 'If life itself is capricious, why should our buildings have any design and any meaning?' So he has pillars that have no purpose. He has stairways that go nowhere. He has a senseless building built and somebody has paid for it."
>
> I said, "So his argument was that if life has no purpose and design, why should the building have any design?" He said, "That is correct."

I then said, "Did he do the same with the foundation?" All of a sudden there was silence. You see, you and I can fool with the infrastructure as much as we would like, but we dare not fool with the foundation because it will call our bluff in a hurry.[9]

What an insightful question. It is the foundations of our culture that are now being weakened by postmodern thinking.

Now more than ever, our culture needs a generation of artists and musicians who desire to reflect God's attributes of beauty and order in fresh and relevant ways. As they arise, they'll find an eager audience, weary of, and left uninspired by, the offerings that have risen from the dead-end worldviews of the last century.

JOURNALISM: IT'S A NEW DAY

The mainstream news organizations in America represent another area in which anti-Christian bias is rampant. David Limbaugh has documented how many key figures in the news business seem blind or indifferent to religious bigotry against Christians, but "seem to perk up when they see opportunities to depict Christians as exclusive, intolerant, and unloving."[10]

Organizations like Brent Bozell's Media Research Center (www.mrc.org) do an outstanding job of monitoring and documenting the bias and distortions that routinely flow from the major news and information outlets in America. The very existence of such organizations has served to provide an important element of accountability that previously didn't exist.

For decades, the news business in this country was dominated by a handful of giants. Three big networks controlled the news on both television and radio. The *New York Times* and *Washington Post* set the agenda for printed news as the AP and UPI fed most newspapers their national news. *Time* and *Newsweek* were the primary players in magazine-based news. Throw in the liberal, government-subsidized

PBS and NPR, and that was pretty much it. It was a small, tight, exclusive little club.

I was in junior high school when our family got its first color television. It was a dramatic improvement over a world that was only seen in black, white, and an infinite variety of shades of gray. There were only three channels available, and to switch from one to the other you had to actually set aside your Dr. Pepper and moon pie (or popcorn made on the stove in a black iron skillet) and get up to turn the knob on the set yourself. Two of our three channels came in clearly, but the other one must have been from Minnesota, because there was always snow on those programs. Our greatest acceleration of convenience when it came to watching TV was the introduction of Jiffy Pop.

Over the past ten to fifteen years, to the dismay of the media news dinosaurs, their monopoly on information distribution has been broken—and with it their ability to steer the national public policy agenda.

First, talk radio on the forgotten AM band began to bring an alternative perspective to huge numbers of Americans. Then, cable news channels and niche magazines began to proliferate. Finally, the Internet became available to most households and represented the final nail in the old news media monopoly's coffin.

Twenty or even ten years ago, Dan Rather and CBS News's *60 Minutes* program would have gotten cleanly away with the fake memo that, only weeks before the general election, claimed to prove that President Bush had shirked his duty with the Texas Air National Guard. A news program would have swung a presidential election—putting John Kerry in office.

But not so in 2004. Within hours of the broadcast, Internet bloggers were pointing out flaws and discrepancies in the memo, which virtually proved it was a forgery. After some initial bluster and denial, CBS had to admit the documents were suspect. Dan Rather's retirement as the face of CBS News was accelerated—though he and his producer continued to argue that the memo was "fake, but accurate."

It is a different day.

Once there were only three or four television channels. Now there are hundreds. This expanded supply of airtime has enabled Christian broadcasters to get out the most important news of all—the Good News of life and wholeness in Jesus Christ. It also has enabled some of us to address news stories that the major press outlets refuse to cover.

For example, on my nationally televised program, *Breakthrough*, I have been able to call attention to the ongoing genocide taking place in Sudan, including the particularly stricken region of Darfur—a story to which the mainstream news organizations have only recently given any attention.

If you do happen to be aware that millions of Christians and animists in southern Sudan have been killed, enslaved, or starved by radical Muslim extremist militias from the north—with either the assent or the aid of the Muslim government there—it's probably *not* because you heard about it through a major news outlet.

As an example of the kind of engagement and outreach I am advocating for all believers and Christian organizations, the Bridge of Hope effort sponsored cooperatively by the church I pastor and the *Breakthrough* television program has helped to purchase the freedom of more than 23,200 Sudanese Christian slaves, who have now been returned to families and loved ones. And it has been our privilege to provide 2.5 million pounds of food and more than $3.25 million worth of medical supplies to the suffering people there, in addition to sending thousands of survival kits to people in danger of death by exposure in that war-torn land.

Needless to say, the days in which a handful of like-minded men can control what does and doesn't become news are over. And that's a good thing for our nation.

At a meeting at World Harvest Church, a conservative commentator and columnist answered a teenage girl's question about how to influence her generation this way: "The most important thing is to get into film making and TV . . . I really think Hollywood is the next frontier."

WHY THE ARTS MATTER

Larry Norman—that great rocker-philosopher of the Jesus Movement—wrote the song "Why Should the Devil Have All the Good Music?" Indeed. Or painting, sculpture, or architecture for that matter. We simply cannot afford to abandon the field where the arts are concerned.

As Nancy Pearcey has written:

Artists are often the barometers of society, and by analyzing the worldviews embedded in their works we can learn a great deal about how to address the modern mind more effectively.[11]

I agree. The Great Commission does not offer us the luxury of simply abandoning the culture to the despair and self-destructiveness inherent in its false worldviews. Our mandate to be salt and light doesn't give us the option of writing people off—including artists.

Francis Schaeffer was spot on when he wrote: "As evangelical Christians, we have tended to relegate art to the very fringe of life. The rest of human life we feel is more important. Despite our constant talk about the Lordship of Christ, we have narrowed its scope to a very small area of reality. We have misunderstood the concept of the Lordship of Christ over the whole of man and the whole of the universe and have not taken to us the riches that the Bible gives us for ourselves, for our lives, and for our culture."[12]

It is time we laid hold of those riches.

ACTION POINTS

- Refuse to abandon the arts to those who reject the God-given values of beauty, order and meaning.
- Support edifying art and artists.
- Encourage talented Christian young people to pursue salt-and-light careers in the fields of the arts and entertainment.
- Send letters of appreciation to actors and entertainers who vocally support the war on terror, our men and women in uniform, and/or their Commander-in-Chief.
- Participate in lively, ongoing online discussions about the intersection of faith and art at www.artsandfaith.com.
- Visit the Media Research Center at www.mrc.org for overwhelming documentation of bias in the news media—including anti-Christian bias.
- Suggested reading:

Art and the Bible, by Francis A. Schaeffer.[13]

Shut Up and Sing: How Elites from Hollywood, Politics, and the UN are Subverting America, by Laura Ingraham.[14]

The Hidden Power of Electronic Culture: How Media Shapes Faith, the Gospel and the Church, by Shane Hipps.[15]

Bias: A CBS Insider Exposes How the Media Distorts the News, by Bernard Goldberg.[16]

eight

THE BATTLEGROUND
OF THE PUBLIC SQUARE

Supposedly, there are two topics polite people don't bring up at social gatherings. They are religion and politics. Perhaps that is why I get such strong reactions from some when, as I have been known to do on occasion, I start talking about both at the same time. As I said in my book *Silent No More*, "In a land where it was once thought rude to discuss religion in public, where men spoke seriously of the death of God, questions of faith now rule the public discourse . . . Our generation is seeking as few others have done in history."[1]

Of course, there are those who think politics is the only topic that I and my fellow evangelicals care about or ever talk about. But that is just a caricature. As the previous and following chapters of this book should demonstrate, the scope of my concern is much, much broader. The fact remains, the Bible and its truth refuse to be isolated in a little religious corner. It speaks with authority to every area of human existence. That surely includes the realm of government and law—sometimes called public policy.

Yes, emotions run high when you wade into the realm of laws and governance. Someone once asked Winston Churchill why he got into politics. He replied, "Ambition. Pure ambition." When then asked why he continued in politics, Churchill said, "Anger. Pure unadulterated anger." Without a doubt, politics is a rough-and-tumble business. It is not for the faint of heart or the thin-skinned.

Some say Christians have no business bringing their faith to the discussion table of public policy at all. Some would even try to tar Christians and radical Muslim extremists with the same brush. They say we would impose an Islamic-style theocracy in America if given the chance.

I have been personally accused of wanting to create a theocracy. There are at least two reasons for this, neither of which have their basis in fact. One is because the Bible and Christian tradition is full of martial language, from the apostle Paul's admonition to put on the armor of God to the old gospel song *Onward, Christian Soldiers*. I have never been afraid to use these examples, nor have I been ashamed of my heritage as a believer in Jesus Christ. We are engaged in warfare, but it is not now nor has it ever been with flesh and blood. Even though those who oppose me may consider themselves to be my enemies, I have never regarded them in that way.

The other reason my words and actions have been misconstrued is because I am determined to attempt to not only stop, but reverse the moral and spiritual erosion that I have seen accelerating so dramatically in my lifetime. In order to do this, I will continue to talk about God in the public square, as many of our Founding Fathers did. The only reason I can imagine that some people become so enraged about this is that they must be afraid of something I am saying, and that fear drives them to take extraordinary measures to stop me from saying it. And this occurs in a land that prides itself on all men having the lawful opportunity to speak freely.

All this fearmongering about the imminent inception of some sort of Christian theocracy imposed by radical right wing clergymen is nonsense.

Nevertheless, after the 2004 elections, *New York Times* columnist Maureen Dowd likened Christian conservatives to "a vengeful mob— revved up by rectitude—running around with torches and hatchets after heathens and pagans and infidels."[2] I take it that Maureen was disappointed by the election returns.

To the charge that Christians want to impose their religious views on others, Catholic scholar Mary Ann Glendon has rightly noted:

> [W]hen people advance their moral viewpoints in the public square, they are not imposing anything on anyone. They are proposing. That's what citizens do in a democracy—we propose, we give reasons, we vote. It's a very strange doctrine that would silence only religiously grounded moral viewpoints.[3]

The inescapable fact is, you can't divorce worldview from public policy and law-making. *Someone's* worldview will inform our laws—it is just a question of *whose*. If not the Christian worldview, then the competing religions of humanism and/or materialism will provide the religious framework for our laws. In fact, they already do to a very large degree. Most of our efforts are merely aimed at recovering a modicum of balance.

"Why not be content to just wall ourselves off from the decaying world and preach to the converted?" some may ask. In other words, "Why fight these battles?"

Martin Luther had a ready answer for that question:

> If I profess with the loudest voice and clearest exposition every portion of the truth of God except precisely that little point which the world and the devil are at that moment attacking, I am not *confessing* Christ, however boldly I may be *professing* Christ. Where the battle rages, there the loyalty of the soldier is proved.[4]

Terrorists commonly use fear, hate, and deception as their weapons. On the other hand, we as believers in Jesus Christ are commissioned to use faith, love, and truth as the weapons that will enable our ideas to prevail in this cultural conflict.

The fact is, there is more than one point at which the world and the devil are attacking our nation in this hour. In the realm of public policy, there are several places in which "the battle rages," and our loyalty as soldiers must be proved. Here are a few of the major ones.

CHURCH-STATE ISSUES

RELIGIOUS FREEDOM

In my previous book, *Silent No More*, I addressed at length the pervasive myth that the First Amendment to the U.S. Constitution demands "separation of church and state." And because it has been so thoroughly and repeatedly debunked by other writers as well, I will not devote a lot of space to it here.

I will say this about it. Though it is a myth, it is one that has been repeated so often, so confidently, by so many, for so long—it is understandable that many Americans have come to believe it is true. What's worse, our federal judiciary has created a significant body of case law that presumes it is true! As a result, church-state issues continue to vex our communities. What's worse, Christians continue to have to fight for the religious freedom the First Amendment actually *does* explicitly guarantee.

To cite just one example, in recent years advocates of religious freedom have had to fight repeated amendments to legislation that would have taken away the rights of churches and religious organizations to consider an applicant's religion in the hiring process. Can you imagine a Baptist charity not being allowed to prefer Baptists, or even Christians, in its hiring?

As the Heritage Foundation has warned, "If any of these amendments were to become law, religious organizations that accept federal funding would be barred from considering the religious beliefs and values of potential employees. No right is more fundamental to preserving religious liberty. Given the size and scope of government, the loss of this protection would signal the decline of a genuinely free and independent civil society."[5]

In a three-part series of articles titled "Religion Under Secular Assault," the *Washington Times* pointed out just how serious and organized are the forces that would push faith and Christian values ever farther away from the center of public life. Speaking of groups like the American Civil Liberties Union (ACLU), People for the American Way, and Americans United for Separation of Church and State, the author wrote:

> They're part of a network of organizations that shares logistics, troops, board members and funding sources and includes radical feminists, humanists, atheists and liberal Jewish and Christian groups. Four organizations furnish most of the leadership.[6]

These groups scan the national landscape looking for opportunities to file lawsuits in the name of "separation of church and state." The focus of these suits ranges from stopping prayers at school sporting events, to having Christian symbols removed from city seals, to keeping nativity scenes off public property at Christmas, to having "under God" removed from the Pledge of Allegiance.

The suits are usually filed with one of two intents—they hope to intimidate the school system or community into stopping the "objectionable" practice through the prospect of an expensive legal battle; or they see the case as a good one for getting a precedent established in the courts.

The secularization of America is well underway. To be sure, through the power of the ballot box we have managed to slow the erosion of our religious freedoms, but greater vigilance and activity on the part of people of faith are required if this troubling trend is to be reversed.

THOUGHT POLICE, AKA "HATE CRIMES" LEGISLATION

Hate crimes legislation is one of those ideas that sounds great at first, sentimental blush (who doesn't want to be against *hate*?), but loses a lot of its appeal once you have a chance to think about it.

Existing federal hate crimes laws create additional penalties for crimes motivated by racial or religious hatred. Many states have passed some form of hate crime legislation as well. As many have pointed out, the problem with these statutes is that they are meant to punish people, not for what they did, but for what they were thinking when they did it. It creates a class of "thought crime."

What concerns many of us who care about religious freedom is where hate crime law will go from here. If Canada and the U.K. are good indicators (and they usually are), we are headed for troubling territory.

In Canada it is currently considered a hate crime to publicly criticize any "identifiable group" such as homosexuals or to assert that homosexuality is wrong. Talk radio hosts and political commentators in that nation must now be hyper-cautious to avoid running afoul of the hate crime laws there. (Conservative talk radio hosts like Rush Limbaugh and even Dr. Laura Schlessinger are blocked in Canada.) In some circumstances it is even illegal to evangelize or "proselytize" in public. After all, telling a non-Christian that Jesus is the only way of salvation is, in a sense, an attack on that person's faith.

Canada's strict hate laws were recently exploited by an Islamic group that wanted to have charges brought against a magazine for "insulting Islam."

Christian groups in Canada are expressing concern that simply reading certain Bible passages aloud may be grounds for prosecution. Regarding the law, Bruce Clemenger, president of the Evangelical Fellowship of Canada, has written: "Now criticism of the redefinition of marriage may be a criminal offense punishable by up to two years in prison. While opposing the promotion of hatred against anyone, we are deeply concerned about the chilling effect this legislation may have on the legitimate expression of religious belief."[7]

And it isn't just Canadian citizens who have need to be concerned. U.S.-based Christian ministries that mail pro-family literature into Canada, as well as those of us who broadcast there, may run afoul of the law as well.

In the U.K. a much-debated "Incitement to Religious Hatred Law" is, as I write, still being negotiated. Christian groups there are deeply concerned that, unless the law is significantly modified, it would also have the effect of muzzling Christians—particularly on subjects such as homosexuality and Islam.

Laws similar to Canada's and Britain's have already been proposed here in the United States. Up to this point, defenders of free speech and freedom of religion have been able to stop them. But ongoing vigilance is necessary.

MARRIAGE AND FAMILY ISSUES

REDEFINING MARRIAGE

The question of what marriage is and who can participate in it took center stage during the 2004 elections. And since then it hasn't shown any tendency toward making an exit or giving up the spotlight.

As I briefly referenced in the previous chapter, the problem with redefining marriage to accommodate gay and lesbian couples who desire the benefits and recognitions afforded traditional couples is that it cannot possibly stop there. Nearly every argument that has been put forth on behalf of gay marriage, if accepted, could then be made with equal force by advocates of other forms of "long-term, committed relationships."

Stanley Kurtz of the Hoover Institution think tank and others have done extensive research on relationship patterns in European countries where marriage has declined, and "civil unions" for homosexuals have been sanctioned. The data show that sanctioning gay marriage is a big step toward the end of marriage as we currently understand it.

In his groundbreaking paper, "Beyond Gay Marriage," Kurtz sounds this sobering note:

> Among the likeliest effects of gay marriage is to take us down a slippery slope to legalized polygamy and "polyamory" (group marriage). Marriage will be transformed into a variety of relationship contracts,

linking two, three, or more individuals (however weakly and temporarily) in every conceivable combination of male and female. A scare scenario? Hardly. The bottom of this slope is visible from where we stand. Advocacy of legalized polygamy is growing.[8]

Is such a complete deconstruction of the meaning of marriage possible? It's closer than you may think. As Kurtz points out, a loose network of organizations that want to see legal recognition for "group marriage" is already in place. "Their cause is championed by a powerful faction of family law specialists . . . Some of these quasi-governmental proposals go so far as to suggest the abolition of marriage," Kurtz warns.[9]

You can be assured Hollywood will continue to do its part to soften up the masses for this sweeping social engineering experiment. In addition to the HBO series *Big Love* I mentioned in the previous chapter, look for additional movies, television series, and documentaries all portraying some form of gay or group marriage in glowingly positive terms.

PARENTS' RIGHTS

Do parents have a right to know what their children have checked out at the public library? Not according to the American Library Association. Do parents have the authority to exempt their children from intrusive school surveys about sexuality? That depends on what state you're in. The same goes for a mom's right to know her daughter is about to undergo a potentially dangerous abortion procedure. On a whole host of issues, the rights of parents to determine significant aspects of their children's upbringing are in jeopardy or already lost.

Animating these efforts to erode parental prerogatives are non-Christian worldviews. As we have seen, some hold that children actually belong to the state, while others assert that children are autonomous and have the same rights and prerogatives as adults.

Hillary Rodham Clinton captured this humanist and statist impulse in the title of her 1996 book, *It Takes a Village: And Other*

Lessons Children Teach Us. The title of the book is derived from the African proverb that states, "It takes a village to raise a child." Of course, Ms. Clinton and her friends at the Children's Defense Fund (where she served as staff attorney at one time) don't have your neighbors and fellow church members in mind when they say "village." As the book makes clear, they're talking about the role of government in overseeing every aspect of a child's upbringing. And where that mission is concerned, parents and their stubborn insistence on having the last say about their kids' upbringing keep getting in the way.

By the way, the topic of Ms. Clinton's thesis at Yale Law School centered on the rights of children. Perhaps that is why, as First Lady, she helped organize opposition in 1996 to a piece of legislation designed to solidify the standing of parents where their children are concerned. It was called the Parental Rights and Responsibilities Act (PRRA).

You can tell quite a bit about a proposed policy by looking at who is lined up against it. In this case, the PRRA attracted a veritable who's who of humanist and secularist organizations—among them, People for the American Way, the ACLU, the National Organization of Women, the Coalition for Reproductive Choice, the National Education Association (NEA), the National Association of School Psychologists, and many others.

This powerful coalition of left-liberal groups threw their combined weight and resources into stopping the legislation—and succeeded. The intensity of their response tells us a great deal about what the cultural elites think of parents' prerogatives and reveals a key component of their strategy for winning the battle for the next generation of Americans.

LIFE ISSUES

PARTIAL BIRTH ABORTION
That the unnecessary and barbaric procedure known as partial birth abortion is still legal in America is a national tragedy.

I don't want to assume you are familiar with the term. At a meeting at World Harvest Church I heard a nationally known Christian artist say that until recently, ". . . I didn't even know what a partial birth abortion was." For those who may not have heard about it, partial birth abortion involves a baby who is completely delivered, except for its head, having its skull punctured by an abortionist and its brain vacuumed into a jar.

I suspect future generations will look back at the culture that rationalized and defended and sanctified this "procedure" and shake their heads in disgusted bewilderment.

In *Silent No More,* I wrote at some length about the devastating effects abortion in general, and partial birth abortion specifically, is having on our national soul. At that time, I wrote:

> It is difficult to see how anyone can fail to understand how a culture that justifies, defends, and institutionalizes such barbarism is in serious jeopardy of stripping away our natural inhibitions against killing in other arenas and spheres. We are excusing what was once inexcusable.[10]

Since I wrote those words, the battle to stop this nightmarish travesty has continued, with precious little to show for it. But that may be about to change.

You may recall that Bill Clinton twice vetoed legislation that would have banned partial birth abortion—though the bills had passed by healthy margins in both houses of Congress. Then in 2000, the U.S. Supreme Court struck down a Nebraska law that would have eliminated the practice in that state. The ruling had the effect of killing similar legislation that was in the works in a dozen other states.

It is interesting to note that the key and deciding vote in that poorly reasoned decision was Sandra Day O'Connor. Upon her retirement in 2005, President Bush nominated John Roberts as her replacement. A short while later, Roberts was nominated and confirmed as Chief Justice after William Rehnquist's death, and Samuel Alito was subsequently nominated for the vacant seat. Both of these men, it is believed, take a dim view of the kind of judicial activism that has consistently kept the citizens from curbing and regulating abortion in the states in which they live.

On November 5, 2003, President Bush did what his predecessor had twice refused to do. I listened intently when he said, ". . . when Congress sends me a bill against partial-birth abortion, I will sign it into law."[11] I consider actions, not just words, as the best indicator of a person's character. I take note of what people say, but then continue to watch to see if they do what they have declared they would do. I was in the room when President Bush signed the Partial Birth Abortion Ban Act (HR 760, S 3). The legislation included an exception for the life of the woman carrying the baby.

Naturally, the act was immediately challenged in federal court by a number of pro-abortion groups in strategically chosen regions of the country. Three federal appeals courts, filled largely with Clinton-appointed judges, ruled the law unconstitutional. Most critical of the law was the notorious Ninth Circuit Court of Appeals in California, the home to some of the most outrageous examples of judicial activism of the last twenty years.

The Bush Justice Department asked the Supreme Court to hear the case, and the high court agreed. Oral arguments were presented in November of 2006, and a ruling is expected in 2007.

Perhaps by the time you are reading this, the new faces on the Court will have swung the balance of power in favor of those who believe that the Constitution means only what it says, and that what it says matters. If so, we will have taken a small, but important step toward restoring some sanity and humanity to our nation's approach to life.

Listen to the story of Gianna Jessen, an abortion survivor, as described in an amicus brief filed with the Supreme Court of the United States by the Center for Moral Clarity in May of 2006:

On April 5, 1977, a pregnant 17-year-old young woman sought a saline abortion at seven months pregnant. The saline abortion procedure involves injecting saline solution into the amniotic fluid. During this abortion procedure, the saline solution burns the fetus and causes it to be delivered dead. This young woman, Tina, was informed by the staff at the abortion clinic that it was in her best interest to obtain an abortion because her mother was already on welfare. Tina and the doctor who injected her abdomen with saline never looked each other in the eye and the doctor only said one word during the entire procedure: "saline." It was a command to the nurse to hand him the saline solution he injected into Tina.

Tina and the other women injected with the solution were required to drink heavy amounts of water and walk around, waiting for their baby to die so that their bodies could discharge it. Tina waited in the clinic overnight. However, something "abnormal" happened. In the early hours of April 6, Tina went into labor. Tina was surrounded by a room full of women who had delivered limp, lifeless babies. Tina, unassisted by any nurse or other worker at the abortion clinic, gave birth to the living baby girl, *amicus* Gianna. Other women were crying, the nurses were shocked.

Gianna was born that morning before the abortionist's scheduled shift. Since the abortionist was not available, Gianna was sent to the hospital, escaping an almost sure death at the hands of the abortionist. She did not completely escape injury from the saline abortion attempt and remained in the hospital for three months. She was later placed with a foster family who specialized in high-risk children.

Due to lack of oxygen supply to her during the abortion, Gianna has been forced to live with cerebral palsy. Although doctors never believed she would be able to sit up or walk, she has exceeded all probabilities. She can now walk *and* run. In April of 2006, she ran in the London marathon. In 1996 and 2000, Gianna testified before Congress concerning her survival of a late-term abortion."[12]

I had the privilege of meeting Gianna, and she is a remarkable young woman—a testimony of the triumph of life over death.

ROE V. WADE

In looking forward from here, it is important for us not to settle for partial victory but continue to press for complete recovery. When David, the future king of Israel, and his men lost their families, homes, and all their possessions to raiders from the south, David asked God two questions: "Shall I pursue my enemies, and shall I overtake them?"

To his surprise, God gave him three answers—"Pursue, overtake, and recover all."

I'm not looking for an America that just gets a little better from here—I want to recover everything we have lost. I'm not just looking for an end to the empires of pornography that objectify women; I'm looking for a society that revolts against the idea of a woman only earning 78 cents compared to every dollar a man makes doing the same job. I refuse to be satisfied with an end to partial birth abortion; I am waiting for the travesty of *Roe v. Wade* to be overturned. I don't want to just see prayer returned to our public schools; I want to see the day when parents can make informed choices about where and how their children will be educated through the implementation of a school choice system.

During the 2005/2006 confirmation hearings of Supreme Court nominees John Roberts and Samuel Alito, you heard a lot from pro-abortion members of the Senate Judiciary Committee about "precedent." In their endless speeches, questions, and statements to the media, they seemed nigh unto obsessed with the topic. To hear them talk, one got the impression that respecting the sanctity of past Supreme Court decisions was the only relevant issue.

You see, the senators had been told in advance that the nominees wouldn't answer questions about how they might vote on cases that were likely to come before the Court. (Just as they shouldn't.) Nevertheless, those pro-abortion senators, and the powerful liberal lobbying groups to whom they are beholden, had only one question on their minds: Would these nominees vote to overturn *Roe v. Wade* if given the opportunity?

Since they couldn't ask that question directly, they decided to go at it another way. Since *Roe v. Wade*—the decision that ripped the delicate and important responsibility of crafting abortion policy away from the states—was an established Court precedent, all they needed were assurances that these prospective new justices would keep existing rulings in place.

There are those who insist that our Constitution is a living document, and because it is alive, it is continually evolving and needs to be reinterpreted according to the times. This is nothing new. Jesus rebuked the religious elites of His day for their modern interpretations, which essentially cancelled the ancient instructions of the law of God. These religious leaders would do anything to enforce their manmade traditions—even to the point of crucifying an innocent teacher from Nazareth.

Before we examine the current situation further, let's take a step back and see how different our history would be if past Supreme Court justices exalted precedent above all other considerations.

In 1896 the U.S. Supreme Court rendered a landmark decision in the case of *Plessy v. Ferguson*. In a 7-1 vote, the justices essentially ruled that states could maintain a racially segregated school system as long as the school facilities provided for blacks were theoretically equal to those provided for whites.

This tragic decision produced the "separate but equal" excuse that made the abhorrent Jim Crow laws possible throughout the South—undoing much of what an ocean of blood had been shed in the Civil War to accomplish.

Now fast forward to 1954. A case challenging the constitutionality of segregated schools has come before the Court. It is the famous *Brown v. Board of Education* case. To rule in favor of Brown and end racial segregation in schools in America will require overturning the precedent of *Plessy v. Ferguson*—which had stood for fifty-eight years! Applying the pro-abortion lobby's newly discovered reverence for precedent, the Court must rule to uphold *Plessy* and allow the injustice of segregation to continue.

Fortunately, the justices didn't. Even though the previous case had been decided by a large majority and had stood for more than five decades, the Court took the opportunity to correct a mistake. And by the way, the Court *does* make mistakes!

For example, the Supreme Court made a huge one in 1857 when it ruled that Dred Scott, a slave, was not a "person" as defined by the Constitution and was therefore not entitled to the protections guaranteed U.S. citizens. Similarly, the Court made a huge mistake when it reasoned in *Roe v. Wade* that an unborn baby isn't a "person" as defined by the Constitution and is therefore not entitled to the protection under the Fourteenth Amendment's promise that no "person shall be deprived of life . . . without due process of law."

Chuck Colson has rightly pointed out the hypocrisy of those who have historically depended upon the willingness of activist judges to overturn precedent in the name of "progressive" change now suddenly becoming champions of respect for precedent. During the Alito hearings, he wrote:

[Respect for precedent] is a matter of prudence, not bedrock principle. As even liberal columnist Michael Kinsley recently pointed out, liberals did not "express any alarm about the danger of overturning precedents" when the Court reversed itself on the issue of gay rights in the *Lawrence* case. The earlier decision, *Bowers*, was as old as *Roe* was at the time of the *Casey* decision.

And when the *Brown* decision outlawed school segregation, "the separate but equal" standard that had been the law of the land for twice as long as *Roe* had been on the books, the Supreme Court rightly reversed it—it was a bad precedent.

As it has throughout its misbegotten existence, *Roe* is the beneficiary of a thinly disguised double standard. If the subject were anything other than abortion, there would be little talk of respecting precedent. On the contrary, the Court would be urged to revisit a wrongly decided case that had caused great harm.[13]

To illustrate that "great harm", let me share with you the story of another victim of a failed abortion attempt from the Center for Moral Clarity's *amicus* brief:

"It is impossible to forget the picture of the little girl missing an arm as the result of a botched late-term abortion. On October of 1991, Rosa Rodriguez, twenty years old at the time, sought a late-term abortion on New York's Lower East Side from abortionist Abu Hayat. Ms. Rodriguez, eight months pregnant, changed her mind and did not want to go through with the abortion. Hayat responded that it was impossible to stop, and that he had to continue. Hayat's assistants held Ms. Rodriguez down while Hayat sedated her.

When she became conscious, she was told the abortion was incomplete and she needed to return. After experiencing increasing pain and bleeding, her mother took her to Jamaica Hospital by taxi. Five hours later, baby Ana Rosa was born. Although Hayat tore off Ana Rosa's right arm, she grew up as a healthy little girl. This healthy baby girl, a teenager by now, will forever be reminded that her arm was pulled from her body due to a late-term abortion."[14]

As you probably know, both Judges Roberts and Alito were confirmed and are now seated on the United States Supreme Court. And with a fresh mix of minds on the Court, the possibility of a reversal of the *Roe v. Wade* decision has entered the minds of many on both sides of the issue.

Of course, pro-abortion forces continually talk as if a reversal of *Roe v. Wade* will instantly make abortion illegal in America. Some of them know better, but I'm sure many have so little understanding of our constitutional process that they actually believe that to be the case.

In reality, a reversal of *Roe v. Wade* will return the power to create laws regulating and/or restricting abortion to the states, where that power lay before. At that point the citizens of those states can go back to doing what the Court has prevented them from doing for more than thirty-three years—that is, prayerfully and painfully attempting to craft laws that are fair, just, and humane.

It is telling that many on the Left speak of the Supreme Court as if it were a legislative body. They have certainly tried to use its power as if it were one. Hopefully, though, we're about to enter a season in which the Court returns to the role designed for it by our wise founders. If we do enter that hoped-for period of restraint, reason, and respect for life, in my opinion it will be because George W. Bush won reelection in 2004 and enough men and women with the right worldview held seats in the United States Senate.

In other words, elections matter a great deal—especially in the battleground of the public square.

ACTION POINTS

- Be prepared to make a strong case for your position on the issues, but always make that case with respect, grace and compassion.
- Support organizations that are fighting for religious freedom and Christians' rights in the nations courts. The American Center for Law and Justice and The Alliance Defense Fund are two of the most prominent.
- Support legislation and constitutional amendments (state and federal) which protect the traditional definition of marriage and the integrity of the family.
- Encourage your representatives to oppose efforts to weaken the rights of parents and support legislation like the Parental Rights and Responsibilities Act.
- Exhort your United States Senators to vote to confirm federal judges who will interpret the Constitution strictly, value the original intent of the framers, and resist legislating from the bench.
- Visit www.CenterForMoralClarity.net, Eagle Forum's Web site, www.EagleForum.com, or Concerned Women for America at www.cwfw.org to stay abreast of important legislation and judicial issues.
- Suggested reading:

The ACLU vs. America: Exposing the Agenda to Redefine Moral Values, by Alan Sears and Craig Osten.[15]

Men in Black: How the Supreme Court Is Destroying America, by Mark R. Levin.[16]

part two

A STRATEGY FOR WINNING

The ragtag Jewish force fanned out across a hill twelve miles outside of Jerusalem at a place called Adasa. Comprised mostly of farmers, priests, and craftsmen, and poorly armed, they numbered no more than a few hundred. Their leader, a rural priest named Judas Maccabeus (known to his followers as "The Hammer") looked across the jagged valley at the well-trained forces of the Seleucid Greeks.

The Greek General Nicanor and more than nine thousand battle-hardened soldiers were arrayed against the Jewish rebels. The year was 161 BC.

This impending battle had been triggered by some of the Jews' refusal to be "Hellenized"—absorbed into the culture of the conquering Greeks. The Greeks worshipped many gods. The Jews, only one. The Greeks had a very loose moral code. The Jews, a very strict and detailed one. It was an irreconcilable clash of worldviews.

The final straw had come a few weeks earlier when the Greek emperor, Antiochus, erected an idol in the Holy Temple—demanding that a Jewish priest sacrifice a pig on the altar in the Most Holy Place and that all the priests bow down to the idol. When a priest was finally found who was willing to commit the abominable sacrifice, Judas killed him on the spot. He then took a hammer and smashed the face of the *idol (earning himself a nickname)—then fled to the hills with his small band of resistors.*

The valley that now stood between Judas's men and the Greek army was the very one that Joshua had used thirteen centuries earlier to pursue the fleeing Amorite kings in the Battle of Gibeon. Perhaps it was the memory of that glorious, God-given victory that filled the rebel hearts with courage as they poured down the hill that day. For before the sun had set, the Greek force had been defeated and scattered. General Nicanor had been among the first of a thousand Greeks to fall.

nine

TOWARD A NEW GREAT AWAKENING

In the early pages of this book, I pointed out that America is not well. That our culture is suffering from a deep and potentially life-threatening moral malaise. And that the only physician who holds a sure cure—the church—is ailing.

The medical metaphor is an apt one, so allow me to extend it. You could consider Part I of this book—the eight chapters you have read thus far—as the *diagnosis* and *prognosis* of the patient. If that is so, then this second part represents the *prescription*.

You see, a diagnosis identifies the problem. A prognosis predicts what the outcome will be if no effective treatment or cure is forthcoming. And a prescription is a course of action for becoming whole and healthy once more. One of the definitions of the Hebrew word "shalom" is "nothing missing, nothing broken." That is what I want to offer you now. It is a prescription for restoring world-changing faith to the church and moral health to our great nation. But Christ is more than just some heavenly pharmacist, sliding a prescription over a counter or through the glass of a drive-through window. He actually comes into our situation and brings the cure He recommends. Or to return to the military theme embodied in the subtitle of this book—I want to show you a strategy for victory, with our

Commander-In-Chief not only directing operations from some ethereal headquarters, but on the ground with us in the thick of the conflict.

Before I could bring that strategy forward, I had to lay the proper groundwork. That meant surveying false worldviews and exposing the seductive lies that have ensnared so many in our generation.

Please understand, we don't embrace a biblical worldview so we can feel smug and superior in our correctness. We do it so we can get down where people are struggling and, from a position of strength, help them. We must possess a clear understanding of the ways in which people are deceived—not so we can condemn them, but so we can reason with them. That, I hope, I have done on the preceding pages.

The Bible declares that the church is in the world, but not of the world; however, we are not separated from the problem—we have been part of the problem. The Jewish exile Daniel prayed and fasted for his people, torn from their land and carried away to Babylon. The ancient prophet Jeremiah wept over his nation and the city of Jerusalem, and although he did not partake of their errors, he identified with them in their departure from God's ways.

In contrast to these examples, Jesus pointed out a sinner and a religious person at the altar. The sinner couldn't even lift up his eyes to God, but simply admitted his sin. The self-righteous religious person was only thankful he was not like the sinner. Far too many within the modern evangelical church have not identified with the man who admitted his guilt, but have too often been perceived as the one who condemned the sinner—this may be the predominant reason why the secular world has found it difficult to hear our message.

THE GREATEST AWAKENING

It is time. That is the message I want you to hear right now. For you, me, and the rest of this generation of slumbering saints—it is time.

It is time for the church to arise—in love, action, and purpose. It is time for God's people to lay aside the weights of self-centeredness and comfort-seeking and shake a nation with an unignorable demonstration of love, power, and service. This is our moment. I like to say, "It's showtime."

We must declare along with the Twenty-fourth Psalm: "This is the generation of those who seek Him, / Who seek Thy face" (v. 6 NASB).

I am convinced that upon certain generations God places "callings." Yes, God deals with and calls individuals to certain endeavors. And yes, from time to time He places a special call upon a local church or a group of churches in a community. But the Scriptures make it clear that God also addresses, calls, and commissions *generations*—just as we saw in the verse above.

Jesus directed some pretty harsh words at the generation of religious leaders in His day:

> But to what shall I liken this generation? It is like children sitting in the marketplaces and calling to their companions. (Matthew 11:16)

> An evil and adulterous generation seeks after a sign, and no sign will be given to it except the sign of the prophet Jonah . . . The men of Nineveh will rise up in the judgment with this generation and condemn it . . . The queen of the South will rise up in the judgment with this generation and condemn it. (Matthew 12:39–42)

> O faithless and perverse generation, how long shall I be with you? (Matthew 17:17)

> For the sons of this world are more shrewd in their generation than the sons of light. (Luke 16:8)

But Jesus made some bold and exciting promises to certain generations as well:

> Assuredly, I say to you, this generation will by no means pass away till all things take place. (Luke 21:32)

Now I believe the Spirit of Jesus Christ has a message for "this generation." There is a call upon this generation of believers. It is a call to be on the forefront of a new great awakening in our nation. It is an awakening that will exceed in strength and scope the sweeping moves of God that have gone before. And make no mistake about it, previous generations of believers have been used of God to effect massive cultural change in a short amount of time.

In the opening years of the twentieth century, a single man of prayer in Wales, Evan Roberts, became a spark that ignited a fire of prayer and fervency in an expanding circle of believers, until the entire nation was engulfed in what came to be known as the Welsh Revival.

Reports from those who witnessed this move of God testify that the Revival changed every aspect of the life across the nation of Wales. As one account described it:

> There was a dramatic decline in drunkenness, bars were deserted as each night the churches were packed with worshippers. The bars were not the only places to be emptied. Dance halls, theaters, and football matches all saw a dramatic decline in attendance. The courts and jails were deserted and the police found themselves without any work to do. Long-standing debts were repaid, church and family feuds were healed and a new unity of purpose was felt across the denominational divides.
>
> Notable among the 150,000 estimated converts of the Revival are George & Stephen Jeffreys who later went on to found the Elim Movement, and David Powell Williams, the founder of the Apostolic Pentecostal church. It is also worth mentioning its effect on Rees Howells, intercessor and founder of the Bible College of Wales and David Lloyd George, who later became the British Prime Minister.[1]

This continent witnessed something very similar early in the eighteenth century. In the 1730s a Scots-Irish immigrant, Reverend William Tennent, and his four sons began praying and preaching revival throughout the colonies. Wherever they went, those who had been ambivalent about faith became committed to it, and those who were ignorant of the condition of their heart became aware of how far away from God they were—and they were prompted to desire a dramatic and life-altering experience of regeneration.

These spiritual pioneers also had the wisdom to invest time and resources in raising up other leaders. By establishing a seminary for training young men in fiery revival preaching, they were able to duplicate themselves many times over. Their preacher school was originally called the Log College. Today it goes by the name Princeton University. Perhaps you've heard of it.

Soon, preachers like Jonathan Edwards, George Whitefield, and John Wesley were turning whole communities upside down for Christ—leaving in their wake hundreds of thousands of new believers who had felt a remarkable touch by God's Spirit.

During the height of the First Great Awakening, the native Englishman George Whitefield was as well known as any man in the American colonies, or the English-speaking world for that matter. It is said that as he preached, rough, hardened, perverse men would cry like infants under the conviction of the Holy Spirit. And upon receiving the gift of forgiveness and salvation, those same men would often shout and run through the aisles or through the streets without the slightest care about what anybody thought.

There is another lesson to be learned in the example of Whitefield. When he made his frequent preaching trips from England to the colonies, he brought more than sermons with him. He brought aid for the poor. As one biographer tells us about Whitefield's work in the young colony of Georgia:

The large audiences in England allowed him to bring many provisions, medicines, and foods with him. His work to distribute them to the poor, and especially to help the orphaned children made a lasting impression on the colony. Georgia was only five years old, and many of the settlers were debtors released from prisons. They were a poor class of settler with no education, no knowledge of farming, and poor health. Many thought the colony would fail. But Whitefield believed otherwise. He brought two teachers with him to establish a school, and urged others to be raised as well.[2]

Here we see a monumental truth we will explore at greater length in the next chapter. Whitefield demonstrated to people that he didn't care only about their souls in the sweet by-and-by. He cared about their empty stomachs in the gritty here and now. He knew a message about the love of God would ring hollow from a messenger who turned an indifferent back on widows and orphans.

Whitefield understood what the second-century church father Tertullian meant when he wrote: "It is our care for the helpless, our practice of lovingkindness that brands us in the eyes of our opponents. 'Look!' they say, 'How they love one another! Look how they are prepared to die for one another.'"

Yes, throughout history nations have seen sudden and dramatic transformations of the culture toward righteousness. So, what can you and I do to trigger the move of God we so desperately need in this crucial hour? The Word of God and history tell us that there are three key ingredients that are precursors to such a spiritual awakening.

A RECIPE FOR RENEWAL

Just as the American colonies' Great Awakening began in just one family and the mighty Welsh Revival in the broken heart of a single man—so, too, our desperately needed move of God will begin with individuals like you and me.

Thus, the first element in preparing for a move of God is *individual moral reform*.

Before our society sees culture-wide revival, we will have experienced private, personal renewal. And personal renewal begins with a reformation of the heart. The old-fashioned Bible word for it is *repentance*. The great evangelist Charles Finney knew a thing or two about revival and repentance. It is he who said, "Revival is a new beginning of obedience to God . . . Just as in the case of a converted sinner, the first step is deep repentance, a breaking down of heart, a getting down in the dust before God, with deep humility and a forsaking of sin."[3] That's not a message you hear much from the pulpit or anywhere else in Christian circles these days. Perhaps that is why we believers seem so impotent to impact a culture that is racing headlong toward destruction.

In the opening chapter I cited a litany of statistics that indicate American Christians are virtually indistinguishable from non-Christians in attitude, practice, and problems. One Christian observer who has seen the data writes: "Whether the issue is divorce, materialism, sexual promiscuity, racism, physical abuse in marriage, or neglect of a biblical worldview, the polling data point to widespread, blatant disobedience of clear biblical moral demands on the part of people who allegedly are evangelical, born-again Christians. The statistics are devastating."[4] Why is this so? At the risk of offending some, I must say that for starters we have too many preachers delivering only what they think people want to hear. And what a lot of people seem to want to hear is nothing more than pop psychology dressed up in religious clothes. In the hope of gathering larger and larger crowds, many are preaching to people's felt needs (what people perceive their needs are) rather than their true needs (the underlying issues in their lives that are the roots of their conflict, dissatisfaction, or lack). We have replaced holiness with humanistic sentiment. We've offered self-help rather than unapologetic calls to self-sacrifice. The hard fact is, you don't sell many sermon CDs when the series title is "Seven Ways to Die to Yourself and Lose Your Life Serving Others." Nevertheless, the first precursor to any culture-wide move of God involves individuals like you and me taking a hard look at our lives and getting things right in repentance and sorrow, just as Charles Finney described.

Some have described it as the taking of a searching and fearless moral inventory of our lives.

I'm talking about having the courage to evaluate not just your behavior, but your motives as well. It is here we must allow God's Spirit to point out those areas of our lives where we've adopted the secular world's way of thinking, acting, and speaking. We admit, with exactness and precision, who we really are; and we allow God to shine His light into all of our hidden corners and do a deep, probing work in our lives.

Colossians 3:5–10 shows us what to look for:

Therefore put to death your members which are on the earth: fornication, uncleanness, passion, evil desire, and covetousness, which is idolatry. Because of these things the wrath of God is coming upon the sons of disobedience, in which you also once walked when you lived in them. But now you must also put off all these: anger, wrath, malice, blasphemy, filthy language out of your mouth. Do not lie to one another, since you have put off the old man with his deeds, and have put on the new man who is renewed in knowledge according to the image of Him who created him.

My wife Joni expressed this very simply—"In retreat, I asked God to show me His glory, and instead He showed me my sin."

Taking moral inventory of your life can be painful. This is especially true if you've been rationalizing and making excuses for a lifestyle of compromise. Back in my native Kentucky, they have a saying for destructive, irrational behavior. They say, "He's snake bit." And in a sense, it's true. We've all been bitten by Satan, the serpent; and there is poison in our souls.

Believers put up with and eventually accept all kinds of addictions, attitudes, and abusive tendencies. Even after our lives have radically changed as a result of accepting Jesus Christ as Savior, the venom of the snake continues to flow through our lives. We deal with the symptoms of our sin, but we don't get to the root of our problems. How do you do that? We join David in praying, "Search me, O God, and know my heart; Try me, and know my anxieties; And see if there is any wicked way in me, And lead me in the way everlasting" (Psalm 139:23–24).

When you get alone with God and allow Him to show you things about yourself, it can be astonishing what He begins to reveal. This private, personal renewal will bring a fresh dimension of God's power and presence in your life. And your family, friends, neighbors, and coworkers will notice. This is how revivals begin.

OVERCOMING "I" TROUBLE

Scan the Bible, human history, and your own heart. You'll find that pride and selfishness are the root of pretty much every ungodly or unholy thing ever done. Pride got the ball rolling back in the Garden of Eden, and it's still the mother of all unrighteousness today.

Jesus made it clear that selfless servanthood was the primary key to influence and leadership: "If anyone desires to be first, he shall be last of all and servant of all" (Mark 9:35). That's why the second key precursor to a new Great Awakening is becoming outwardly focused rather than inwardly obsessed. Sadly, that latter term describes a significant majority of American believers today.

According to British theologian John Stott, somewhere along the line today's evangelicals became "more and more associated with self-absorbed individuals preoccupied with finding health and happiness for their own lives and maintaining the status quo in an unstable world. As this concern for the individual increased, concern for society at large correspondingly decreased."[5] A whole generation of believers has largely become "I" focused—consuming massive amounts of preaching and teaching on how to be happier, healthier, wealthier, skinnier, prettier, and more fulfilled.

How could this have happened? I believe it is because of a wholesale neglect of the preaching of the cross. The New Testament's presentation of the cross describes more than just the place where Jesus effects our redemption. It is a place where the Jesus-follower comes to die to self.

Then Jesus said to His disciples, "If anyone desires to come after Me, let him deny himself, and take up his cross, and follow Me. For whoever desires to save his life will lose it, but whoever loses his life for My sake will find it." (Matthew 16:24–25)

As I have mentioned before, self-denial is entry level Christianity. The cross is not a place of exaltation, it is a place of shame and ridicule. We want to wear it as a decoration, but fail to recognize it is a place of denial. The One who hung there was rejected by everyone, but instead of identifying with Him we insist on being accepted by everyone.

"Let him deny himself . . ." "Whoever loses his life . . ." Those are not messages that win preachers popularity contests. So while America's liberal churches have abandoned the preaching of the cross because of its focus on sin and repentance, many of her conservative evangelical churches have shied away from it because of its unpopular call for self-denial and sacrifice.

The very way we have brought new Christians into the kingdom has set us up for this tragic, influence-robbing pattern of self-absorption. When we begin with the message, "God loves you and has a wonderful plan for your life," should we be surprised that many enter the kingdom thinking, *Of course, it's all about me*?

Is it any wonder most evangelical churches today can't even get people to work in the nursery once a month—much less reach out to drug addicts or struggling single mothers? They have never been told that to save your life, you must lose it.

The culture-transforming revivals of the past were fueled by the whole gospel preached unapologetically by men like Whitefield and Finney. It was both a spiritual gospel and a social gospel. It pointed men to worship of God *and* service to others. But as Pastor Robert Lewis has pointed out, the two halves of the gospel message got separated along the way:

Most of the twentieth century was a story of separation. Of an either/or Christianity. Either a social gospel *or* a spiritual gospel. Either a horizontal construct emphasizing human compassion *or* a vertical construct emphasizing amazing grace. But isn't the cross a powerful combination of both? The horizontal *and* the vertical? Isn't the cross, in fact, a bridge, uniting supernatural and human realities?[6]

It is, indeed. Lewis accurately sums up the tragedy when he points out, "[O]ur rich heritage of influencing society through humble acts of charity, strategic community concern, and sacrificial works of service has been largely forsaken and has been replaced by a one-sided gospel of proclamation."[7] We must remerge the two halves of the gospel message. Beginning with you and me, we must take hold of contemporary problems with passion, love, and truth—including issues that may be well outside our comfort zones. Some problems will lie close to home (pornography addiction, the high divorce rate, rampant teenage promiscuity, and responsible stewardship of the environment). Others may be quite distant (African genocide of Christians, religious persecution in China, and government-induced famines in Zimbabwe).

Influence comes through service, and a self-absorbed people are incapable of serving.

In the Old Testament book of 2 Kings, chapter 7, four lepers sat at the gate of Samaria, which was shut up because of a siege. God intervened on behalf of His people, and caused the besieging Syrian army to flee in terror, although those behind the city walls knew nothing of their change of fortune. Meanwhile, the starving lepers finally decided to give themselves up to their enemies. To their great surprise, they found all the Syrian's tents empty, with all their possessions left behind. The lepers' first reaction was to eat and drink their fill and carry away as much plunder for themselves as they could. They literally became exhausted in their efforts at self-fulfillment. They finally realized their fault, and went back to the city to share the good news that the siege had been lifted.

What a picture of the present me-centered generation, worn out with self-absorption! Millions are starving for a morsel of natural and spiritual bread, and we have more than enough, but fail to recognize our responsibility to share our abundance.

The good news is, God's Word contains some wonderful promises for those who will deny themselves and become outwardly focused. All the riches and resources of heaven itself are available to the one who gives and serves. As 2 Chronicles 16:9a tells us: "For the eyes of the LORD move to and fro throughout the earth that He may strongly support those whose hearts are completely His" (NASB).

And it is just such a people who will trigger the renewal our nation so urgently needs.

"IF MY PEOPLE . . ."

The final and most widely acknowledged precursor to culture-shaking revival is *prayer*. I said it is widely acknowledged. I did not say it is widely practiced.

Fervent, soul-wrenching intercession for our communities and nation is practically a lost artifact of a previous day—a day in which Christians spent significant seasons of time praying for things other than themselves and their immediate felt needs.

The predominant prayer request we received on our national telephone prayer line years ago was for the salvation of family members. Today the top three categories of requests for prayer all deal with personal needs. Salvation for family members has dropped all the way to eighth place. This is just another indicator of how self-centered we have become.

As I mentioned previously, Evan Roberts is credited by history as being the spark that ignited the Welsh Revival. Roberts was neither a high-powered preacher nor a great theologian. He had never been to Bible college or seminary. In fact, he had left school at the age of eleven to help his father in the local coal mine. He was not an eloquent speaker or a philosopher. He was a coal miner. He was, however, one who loved Jesus passionately and who, in prayer, caught hold of Christ's heart for hurting, hopeless people.

At the age of about fifteen, Roberts began studying the great revivals of history. Not long after, he started praying—often in tears and anguish—to see one in his nation and in his time. At twenty-six, Roberts would write, "For ten or eleven years I have prayed for revival . . . I could sit up all night to read or talk about revivals."[8] What Roberts and others began in their prayer closets, the Spirit of God ratified and continued by pouring Himself out on a nation. Hundreds of thousands found peace in this life and a heavenly home in the next—because of prayer.

We need to pray for our president and other leaders in government—as the Scriptures explicitly command us to do. But go a step further. Ask the Holy Spirit to reveal to you key individuals in the realms of politics, the arts, or athletics for whom you should intercede. Then prepare to be amazed as you see those prayers bear fruit.

Your prayers could alter the course of our nation. I have no doubt about that. Moses prayed and rescued his people from certain destruction. Elijah prayed the northern kingdom of Israel back from the brink of annihilation. John Knox prayed and shook the very throne of Scotland. There are legacies yet to be written through the effectual, fervent prayers of the righteous.

Pray. Lay hold of God's highest willingness to restore our nation in these pivotal days of history. Pray until principalities and powers are shaken. Pray until heaven touches the earth. Pray until your heart beats to heaven's pulse. Pray and prepare to be amazed at what God will do *in* you, and then *through* you.

IT CANNOT FAIL

I opened this chapter by pointing you to Psalm 24:6: "This is the generation of those who seek Him, / Who seek Thy face."

I believe we are that generation. I believe this is our time. I think the great Bible teacher R. A. Torrey had all this in mind when he said:

I can give a prescription that will bring revival . . . to any church, or community, or any city on earth. First: Let a few Christians get thoroughly right with God. If this is not done, the rest will come to nothing. Second: Let them bind themselves together to pray for revival until God opens the windows of heaven and comes down. Third: Let them put themselves at the disposal of God for His use as He sees fit in winning others to Christ . . . That is all. It cannot fail.[9]

Look again at Torrey's third point—putting ourselves "at the disposal of God for His use as He sees fit." What might that look like? What might a loving Father who sacrificed His own Son for mankind see fit for us to do? The answer lies ahead.

ACTION POINTS

- Follow the example of George Whitefield. Be ready to minister to people's material needs as you endeavor to speak to their spiritual needs.
- Take the three prerequisite steps for personal revival:
  1. Repentance resulting in personal moral reform.
  2. Becoming outwardly focused rather than inwardly obsessed.
  3. Pray. Begin now to pray for revival—a mighty wave of spiritual awakening and renewal—in America.
- Visit www.revival-library.org and read about many nation-shaking revivals throughout history.
- Suggested reading:

Forgotten Founding Father: The Heroic Legacy of George Whitefield, by Stephen Mansfield.[10]

Fire on the Altar: A History and Evaluation of the 1904-05 Welsh Revival, by Noel Gibbard.[11]

ten

A CALL TO COMPASSION AND ACTION

Imagine for a moment you have never before read the Bible or heard any teaching from it. Then one day, a Bible drops out of the sky onto your lap, and you proceed to read it front to back. What impressions or information about God would you take away from that reading? If someone said, "Tell me about this God of the Bible," what would you tell him you had learned?

After just one pass, you might not deduce the mystery of the Trinity, or the nuanced theological distinctions between God's *immanence* and *omnipresence*. You might not notice the paradox of God's sovereignty over a people He endows with free will. But there is one thing about God I'm almost certain you would understand clearly:

God cares deeply about orphans, widows, and the poor, and expects His people to share His concern.

You wouldn't have to be some sort of theological prodigy to pick up that truth. In fact, any child would discern it, for it is stated clearly and repeatedly from one end of the book to the other.

Take Job, for example, which is widely understood to be the first book of the Bible to be written. You'll recall that Job was the man God pointed to as the finest example of what a human being could be.

When the devil walked into God's throne room and began to vilify humanity, God essentially pulled out His wallet and showed him a picture of Job, saying, "Have you seen my boy? He's amazing!"

> Then the LORD said to Satan, "Have you considered My servant Job, that there is none like him on the earth, a blameless and upright man, one who fears God and shuns evil?" (Job 1:8)

That is quite an endorsement, considering the source. Have you ever wondered what it was about Job's character and behavior that merited such a stunning assessment from God? We don't have to speculate. Let's interview Job to get it directly from his mouth.

"Job, our first question for you is: God clearly considers you uniquely 'blameless and upright' among all the people of the earth. Why do think that is?"

> Because I delivered the poor who cried out,
> The fatherless and he who had no helper.
> The blessing of a perishing man came upon me,
> And I caused the widow's heart to sing for joy . . .
> I was eyes to the blind,
> And I was feet to the lame.
> I was a father to the poor,
> And I searched out the case that I did not know.
> I broke the fangs of the wicked,
> And plucked the victim from his teeth. (Job 29:12–17)

"I see. So, you made a lifestyle out of aiding orphans, widows, the disabled, the poor, and the victimized. Well, some friends of yours have speculated that you must have committed a terrible sin. Otherwise you wouldn't have hit that really rough patch in your life a while back. What do you consider sinful, and how do you respond to that suggestion?"

If I have kept the poor from their desire,
Or caused the eyes of the widow to fail,
Or eaten my morsel by myself,
So that the fatherless could not eat of it . . .
If I have seen anyone perish for lack of clothing,
Or any poor man without covering;
If his heart has not blessed me,
And if he was not warmed with the fleece of my sheep;
If I have raised my hand against the fatherless,
When I saw I had help in the gate;
Then let my arm fall from my shoulder,
Let my arm be torn from the socket. (Job 31:16–22)

"Interesting. So you think the most offensive thing a person could do before God would be to turn an indifferent back on people in need. Well, thanks for your time."

The Bible's unifying theme of compassion doesn't end in Job. When God was giving the nation of Israel specific instructions about how to form a godly society in the land of promise, He built consideration for orphans and widows right into the laws of the land. For example, in Leviticus 19, God commands the Israelites not to harvest the grain in the corners of their fields, but rather to leave it for "the poor and the stranger" (v. 10). In the book of Ruth, we find the widows Ruth and Naomi benefiting from this benevolent practice in the fields of righteous Boaz.

In Deuteronomy, God establishes a law by which the Israelites are to set aside a significant portion of their produce every third year. This reserve is designed to support the priests as well as "the stranger and the fatherless and the widow who are within your gates, [that they] may come and eat and be satisfied, that the LORD your God may bless you in all the work of your hand which you do" (Deuteronomy 14:28–29).

Notice the promise of heavenly blessing for those who will be obedient in this way. This is something we'll see God repeating through His

Word. In fact Psalm 41 lists seven special blessings God bestows upon those who refuse to turn a blind eye to the want and lack of others:

> Blessed *is* he who considers the poor;
> The LORD will *deliver him* in time of trouble.
> The LORD will *preserve him* and *keep him alive,*
> And he will be *blessed on the earth;*
> You will *not deliver him to the will of his enemies.*
> The LORD will *strengthen him* on his bed of illness;
> You will *sustain him* on his sickbed. (Psalm 41:1–3, emphasis added)

In another psalm, God declares Himself a "father of the fatherless" and a "defender of widows" (Psalm 68:5). Similar statements are made throughout Proverbs and the prophetic books as well. For example, in Isaiah, God commands His people to "rebuke the oppressor; defend the fatherless, plead for the widow" (Isaiah 1:17; see also Isaiah 58:6–7).

We all know that Sodom is described in the Bible as one of the most appallingly wicked and depraved cultures in history. And everyone *thinks* he knows the sin that made God feel it necessary to wipe out the city completely. In the book of Ezekiel, God, speaking in the first person to corrupt Jerusalem, tells us plainly what made Sodom and her "daughter," Gomorrah, so offensive:

> Look, this was the iniquity of your sister Sodom: She and her daughter had pride, fullness of food, and abundance of idleness; neither did she strengthen the hand of the poor and needy. And they were haughty and committed abomination before Me; therefore I took them away as I saw fit. (Ezekiel 16:49–50)

I think we all know what the "abomination" they committed was. But notice that it is not the first thing God mentions. At the top of the list is (paraphrasing here) "being overfed and comfortable while ignoring the poor." That is not to suggest that the practice of homosexuality is not offensive in the eyes of God. Far from it. And, I should also point out that it is not wrong to enjoy the blessings of God while you minister to the poor. But absorbing the truth of this passage makes me deeply concerned about our country, and more to the point, the church in this country. Is it possible that God is more dismayed by the widespread indifference to the poor displayed by most Christians than the fact that *Will & Grace* reruns are popular on television? This passage would suggest it is. What a tremendous example for us to be faithful, not only in righteousness issues, such as the protection of marriage, but in justice issues, such as the relief of poverty!

Sodom became synonymous with self. And the more self-focused a person becomes, the more likely it is that they will become satiated with ordinary diversions and continue to digress further and further into debauchery and degradation.

I remember attempting to stay awake after a traditional Kentucky Thanksgiving dinner years ago. It was while I was in a tryptophan-induced haze that it occurred to me that lethargy and slumber invariably follow overeating. The most common cure was and is to get up and keep moving. Is it possible that the root of the church's current sleepy state is that we've gorged ourselves on the abundant blessings available to us? I submit to you that we've eaten too much and served too little.

When you move into the New Testament, the Bible's emphasis on concern for the poor is only amplified. I could cite numerous statements of John the Baptist, Paul, and especially Jesus. But for the sake of brevity, I will mention only one—Jesus' sobering parable of the sheep and the goats. Before I do, let me remind you again of something I wrote in *Silent No More*:

Like honoring our parents, caring for the poor is a command with a promise. The Bible tells us that if we would uphold the mandate to be generous to the poor, we would ourselves be happy (Prov. 14:21), God would preserve us (Ps. 41:1-2), we would prosper and be satisfied (Prov. 11:25), and we would be raised up from beds of affliction (Ps. 41:3). All throughout the Scriptures, Christians are reminded that care for the needy is at the heart of true faith. Thus it has always been the aspiration of faithful churches to be "zealous for good works" (Titus 2:14).[1]

The King of kings, referring to His end-time Throne of Judgment, said:

> All the nations will be gathered before Him, and He will separate them one from another, as a shepherd divides his sheep from the goats. And He will set the sheep on His right hand, but the goats on the left.
>
> Then the King will say to those on His right hand, "Come, you blessed of My Father, inherit the kingdom prepared for you from the foundation of the world: for I was hungry and you gave Me food; I was thirsty and you gave Me drink; I was a stranger and you took Me in; I was naked and you clothed Me; I was sick and you visited Me; I was in prison and you came to Me."
>
> Then the righteous will answer Him, saying, "Lord, when did we see You hungry and feed You, or thirsty and give You drink? When did we see You a stranger and take You in, or naked and clothe You? Or when did we see You sick, or in prison, and come to You?"
>
> And the King will answer and say to them, "Assuredly, I say to you, inasmuch as you did it to one of the least of these My brethren, you did it to Me." (Matthew 25:32–40)

Of course, the "King" in this parable then turned his attention to the "goats." Because they failed to offer food, water, clothing, or comfort to "the least of these," they received less pleasant instructions. "Depart from Me . . . ," they were told.

What a sobering thought, indeed.

THE POWER OF COMPASSIONATE SERVICE

Please understand, I am not remotely interested in *scaring* you into being more generous toward the poor. Nor do I desire to make you feel some sort of joyless, legalistic obligation to support widows and orphans. I just want you to see what God considers important because I know people who love God and want to please Him will become passionate about the things He is passionate about. Furthermore, as we saw in the previous chapter, hands-on ministry to the lowest strata of society is a major key to unleashing a wave of renewal and revival in our nation. It is the neglected half of the gospel message that shook nations in centuries past.

I know it has become a syrupy cliché, but the saying is true just the same: "People don't really care what you know until they know you care."

We in the church have spent much breath and spilled a river of ink letting prostitutes, alcoholics, and fatherless young gang members know what the Bible says about their lifestyles. But have we been equally active in finding ways to let them know that God loves them desperately and wants them to be whole and at peace? Have we been so concerned about being *correct* that we have failed to *connect*? Francis Schaeffer said, "Biblical orthodoxy without compassion is surely the ugliest thing in the world."[2]

Baptist writer Henry Blackaby, referring to the church's lack of moral integrity, has said, "Our gospel is cancelled by the way we live." This is a point I made in the previous chapter. But I would add that our gospel is also cancelled by the way we *serve*—which is to say, too little and too rarely.

This is something we have made mighty efforts to correct in the church I pastor. I say this not to boast but to offer an example of what I'm encouraging. Several years ago we established our Bridge of Hope initiative that, from its inception, was designed to present both halves of the gospel to "the least of these" all over the world and right here in America.

Through Bridge of Hope, we have been active in Sudan where the government's atrocious human rights record, an active slave trade victimizing mostly Christian men, women, and children, the Sudanese government's use of militia and other forces to support slave raiding, and the aerial bombardment of civilian targets had all combined to create a catastrophe of human suffering and genocide.

As I mentioned in a previous chapter, it has been our privilege to be instrumental in freeing 23,200 Sudanese Christian slaves. In addition, Bridge of Hope has provided the funds to rush 2.5 million pounds of food, more than $3.25 million worth of medical supplies, and more than 6,000 "survival kits" to suffering people there. And as I write, we have completed two medical clinics in Sudan that will double as churches and distribution centers for ongoing relief.

In Nicaragua, Kosovo, Venezuela, Mozambique, El Salvador, and tsunami-ravaged southern Asia, Bridge of Hope has combined the meeting of immediate material needs with the sharing of the message of eternal life in Christ—just as George Whitefield modeled for us more than 250 years ago, and as Jesus modeled for us with the feeding of the five thousand!

Here at home, Bridge of Hope has helped provide more than one million pounds of food to families in cities across America who are struggling to make ends meet. We have rushed 2.7 million pounds of clean water, food, and supplies to families impacted by Hurricanes Katrina and Rita. We also provided assistance to communities in southeastern West Virginia that were severely damaged by flooding on two separate occasions just a few months apart.

In addition, as a result of another one of our outreaches called Reformation Ohio, we have partnered with other churches and ministries to present the gospel of Jesus Christ personally to over 175,000 people, feed 25,000 families, and record over 18,000 salvations in our home state. And all of this was accomplished by the grace of God in just one year!

These are just a few examples of the kinds of things that can be accomplished from those who recognize their responsibility to obey biblical instruction. Certainly, I am aware there are many churches and organizations that are doing similar work. I'm so thankful they are. But to my sorrow, I am also aware of the statistics that show how little the average American Christian gives in terms of resources or time toward ministry to the destitute and hurting.

George Barna's research shows that only six in every one hundred born-again Christians even tithe, or give a tenth of their income to God's work.[3] In fact, another long-term study shows that the average church member in America gives only about 2.6 percent of family income to the local church.[4] And giving to nonchurch organizations that care for orphans, widows, and the poor is even lower. The numbers tell a shameful story—as the average income of Americans has increased, their spending on anyone but themselves has plummeted.[5]

I am compelled to ask: How is God going to use us to impact a generation if He can't even get us to be obedient with finances?

MAKING IT PERSONAL

Tithing to the local church and giving generously to Christian humanitarian organizations should really be only the starting point for a believer who is passionate about honoring God and following Jesus. The real power to transform our culture lies in individuals personally "getting their hands dirty" in direct service where they live and work.

Bob Lewis, pastor of Fellowship Bible Church in Little Rock, Arkansas, has well-developed programs in his church designed specifically to equip and encourage individuals to launch out into this kind of personal, hands-on ministry. Why? As he explains in his book *The Church of Irresistible Influence*:

> [I]n the journey of spiritual life, one matures fully, not just with growing and learning but with serving. The Christian life is intended to crescendo around each person finding his or her place in the constantly unfolding pattern of kingdom work that engages the unique gifts and abilities with which each person has been endowed by God.[6]

Where should you begin? How about at home? As Chuck Colson has observed, "The family is often described as a 'school of charity,' in the sense that it's the easiest place to learn how to give ourselves to others . . . We sometimes do extraordinary things for the sake of our spouses and children. And in this process of learning the lessons of charity, we may find that living for others makes life worthwhile."[7]

The next obvious frontier for service is your own neighborhood. We seem to live in a time in which few people actually *know* their neighbors anymore. Yet within walking distance of your home, you are likely to find desperate hurts and crisis-level needs. Why not start praying that God would show you opportunities for service and sharing among your neighbors? It's really not as hard as you may think. In two outreach campaigns, our church members made personal contact with 15,000 homes—the equivalent of many entire communities.

Of course, a short drive away from the typical, tidy suburban street lined with manicured lawns and well-appointed houses, you'll find another kind of neighborhood. One where the houses aren't so nice and the cars aren't so shiny and new. Here you'll find no shortage of needs to meet and wounds to heal.

Fatherlessness is a huge problem everywhere in America, but particularly so in many inner-city neighborhoods. The women and children involved are really just a form of the "widows and orphans" the Bible so strongly encourages us to consider and help. Name a social ill or negative outcome—illiteracy, disease, crime, violence, addiction, or prison—and it will be appallingly high among these families.

What can one person or even one church do to combat such pervasive and deeply entrenched problems? You would be surprised. Here are a few of the ministries available at the church I am privileged to pastor, World Harvest Church in Columbus, Ohio:

Bethany Place: A safe and nurturing environment designed especially for families of children with disabilities. Parents can attend church while their kids are in Bethany Place, knowing they are receiving compassionate care from conscientious and qualified caregivers.

Canaan Land: One of only three handicapped-accessible playgrounds in central Ohio, designed so children with disabilities can make full use of the equipment.

Hands for the Harvest: A dedicated group of volunteers who translate every service and most special events into American Sign Language for those who are hearing impaired.

Chariots of Fire: Specially trained volunteers who assist those with handicaps who visit or attend our church.

Latin Harvest: A church dedicated to reaching the Latin community in central Ohio, with church services in Spanish, outreach, home groups, and projects of compassion.

Metro Harvest: A significant investment into our community with weekly meetings, instructional classes, Hope Centers in economically disadvantaged neighborhoods, and transportation to church services. Some of the weekly instruction available at two locations in our city include: Substance Abuse Recovery, GED Classes, Computer Training, Financial Management Classes, and English as a Second Language.

This is just a sampling of the opportunities for ministry available to those in our community. I also need to mention some of the other ministries in which we are involved:

Breakthrough: A worldwide media ministry that reaches 97 percent of the homes in America, 78 percent of Canada, and over 150 nations of the world. *Breakthrough* is also responsible for printed, audio, and video materials which are sent worldwide. We also maintain a 24-hour prayer center which is literally an altar for the nation.

Bridge of Hope: As I have already outlined, we are proud to partner with some of the finest missions organizations on the planet to provide relief to suffering humanity around the globe.

The Center for Moral Clarity: A nationwide ministry where we believe righteousness can be exalted in our nation through prayer, information, and action. CMC has been instrumental in key struggles for reclaiming our culture, such as encouraging believers to speak out about partial birth abortion, confirmation of Supreme Court nominees, and more.

World Harvest Church Ministerial Fellowship: A fellowship of like-minded ministers who have joined together for instruction, inspiration, and impartation. The fellowship represents over 2,000 ordained and licensed ministers from all 50 states and 42 nations.

World Harvest Bible College: Known as the School of the Spirit, WHBC enrolls hundreds of students each year to be trained to go into the harvest fields with the message of reconciliation and restoration. Graduates have literally gone worldwide, from remote villages in third world countries to staff positions with some of the most powerful people in the world. Another outreach of the Bible College is **Remnant**, a group of young people who are redeeming the arts through drama, dance, mime, and song.

Harvest Preparatory School: A preschool through 12th grade program that gives inspiration, education and hope to students from 13 school districts and 62 local churches in a seven-county area. Many of these children were struggling in their previous schools, and have found success academically, athletically, and spiritually at HPS. Seniors at HPS are involved in **Just Cause**, a service organization that ministers to homeless families in Columbus. Each year, the senior class includes missions outreach as part of their senior experience.

Reformation Ohio: An organization comprised of churches, businesses and individuals who preach the gospel, initiate programs of compassion, and register voters across Ohio, predominantly in communities that have experienced economic hardship.

What you and other like-hearted believers can do in your community is really limited only by your imagination and the depth of your compassion. I can promise you one thing. As you become less self-focused and begin pouring yourself into the lives of others through service, you'll experience more blessing, fulfillment, and joy than you've ever known.

FAITH-BASED OPPORTUNITIES

One of the first things President George W. Bush did upon entering office in January 2001 was to keep his campaign promise to open a White House Office of Faith-Based and Community Initiatives. At the same time he signed an executive order that instructed the distributors of federal grant money to stop discriminating against religious organizations. In the president's words: "I wanted to make sure that the faith-based groups simply got equal access and equal treatment when it came to the billions of dollars we spend at the federal level."[8]

For decades, religious charities and community groups were passed over as federal agencies handed out billions of dollars to secular groups with similar missions. The same twisted understanding of "separation of church and state" that has created so much fear and misinformation in the public schools had kept many of America's most effective and efficient outreaches from accessing badly needed funds—simply because their programs were Christian in nature. At the same time, humanism has become a religion in its own right—virtually the only religion that is allowed in most public institutions in America.

All that changed with the Bush presidency. Since he took office, billions of federal dollars have flowed to ministries and charities working in the trenches to help the poor, unwed mothers, fatherless kids, and so much more. For example, in the year 2004, nearly $20 billion in competitive grants was handed out by seven different federal agencies. And a full $2 billion of that went to faith-based organizations.

In that same year, standing before a group of several hundred leaders of faith-based organizations, President Bush said:

The question this administration is asking is simply, "Are you getting results?" That's all we care about. Are you meeting the standards of your church and the government, and are you getting results? If you say, "Yes," then the federal government, rather than being fearful of you, ought to say, "Thank you. Thank you for doing your mission to change the United States of America."

Do you find that as refreshing as I do? It really is a new day in terms of Christian organizations being able to partner with the government to help people in meaningful ways, without having to hide or subordinate the distinctive Christian character of their efforts. Hopefully, that new day will continue beyond President Bush's tenure through the election of a like-spirited successor.

There has been growing concern among some about the activities of churches and other tax-exempt organizations, especially when it comes to their involvement in issues affecting public policy or other matters of the marketplace. Until 1954, there was no federally mandated constraint upon what a church or a minister could advocate from the pulpit. Everything changed as a result of a provision attached to a tax bill proposed by Lyndon B. Johnson (then a member of the U. S. Senate), which required tax-exempt organizations to limit their so-called "political activity." What this effectively did was to muzzle clergymen from speaking to issues that affected not only their churches, but their communities and their culture. Unfortunately, these constraints are becoming more and more stringent.

The reason churches and similar organizations were given exemption from taxation in the first place was not so that they would become silent regarding political issues, but because of the money they saved the government through their charitable, humanitarian, and community work. The investment that churches and other organizations make in these kinds of efforts is incalculable, and it is going on in cities and communities across the nation and the world.

Among the many faith-based initiative success stories I could cite, Kids Hope USA is a notable example. This is an amazing organization that helps churches recruit and match Christian adults for long-term mentoring relationships with at-risk elementary school children. The model for the amazing success of this ministry is one school, matched with one church, that connects one caring mentor with each struggling child. The results are astounding. Here is how a pastor described his church's involvement in Kids Hope USA:

> If there is any ministry we undertake at our church that embodies the Easter message of God's power to renew and give hope, KIDS HOPE USA has to be it.
>
> We help make every day Easter for a child in need. A little first grader called Annie comes to mind. Her home situation is difficult. Five males in her family are in prison at the moment and she is being raised by her grandmother. When school began, she was extremely withdrawn, making no eye contact, having little social interaction, and doing very little school work. Today, Annie's KIDS HOPE USA mentor is looking for extra enrichment activities for her, because she is performing above the class average in all her subjects.[9]

As Jesus said, "Whatever you have done for the least of these . . . you have done for Me." Now, through the White House Faith-Based Initiatives, some of the tax dollars American Christians pay each year are being returned to make that kind of ministry possible.

THE BIG QUESTION

At the heart of this chapter is a question: Why are you here?

There is a reason you were born in this extraordinary moment in history. There is a high and holy purpose behind your existence. That you are drawing breath as you read this line is a fact saturated in divine meaning and method. And whether you know it or not, the stewardship you exercise over your brief journey on this earth carries eternal implications—for you and for many others.

You fulfill your God-ordained purpose through a series of seemingly insignificant events. These events can and should result in a passionate pursuit of that for which God created you.

I can't know the specifics of that purpose. But I do know it generally. You are here to extend God's redemptive love to others. To place the jewel of a soul in the crown of our Savior—that the Lamb of God slain may receive the reward of His suffering and sacrifice.

We are called to influence. Whether that translates into getting involved in a faith-based outreach like Kids Hope USA, sharing financial support with a global outreach like Bridge of Hope, or simply delivering a hug and a Wal-Mart gift card to a single mother whose kids need winter coats—you and I cannot possibly walk in God's high purposes while we seek only our own comfort.

We must resist the worldview that seductively pulls toward selfishness and self-absorption.

ACTION POINTS

- Find creative ways to bring meaningful help to widows, orphans and the poor.
- Put your money where God's heart is. Direct at least 10 percent of your income toward the work of your local church and faith-based organizations serving "the least of these" like Kid's Hope USA (www.KidsHopeUSA.org)
- Support Christian humanitarian outreaches like Bridge of Hope (www.breakthrough.net/bridge.asp), Franklin Graham's Samaritan's Purse (www.samaritanspurse.org), or Charles Colson's Angel Tree Network (www.angeltree.org).
- Get your hands dirty doing real service in your neighborhood or your community. Volunteer at in inner city mission. Help a single mom. Teach an illiterate adult to read. The opportunities are endless.
- Suggested reading:

The Church of Irresistible Influence, by Robert Lewis with Rob Wilkins.[10]

Freedom, Justice and Hope: Toward a Strategy for the Poor and the Oppressed, by Marvin Olasky, et. al.[11]

Renewing American Compassion: How Compassion for the Needy Can Turn Ordinary Citizens into Heroes, by Marvin Olasky.[12]

eleven

FIGHTING FOR THE LIFE
OF A DYING CULTURE

This book is built upon a martial metaphor. The very subtitle carries the word war. But as I said in the introduction, I write of a different kind of conflict. It is not a conflict of guns, but of ideas; one in which the fight is for institutions, not territory; hearts, not hills. It is a clash of paradigms, value systems, and visions of the future—a war for the soul of our nation. In the face of this conflict, the response recommended by some in the body of Christ has simply been: *retreat*. "If the country is determined to go to hell in a handbasket, let it," seems to be the attitude. "As long as we're free to worship as we choose, who cares what they do?" others say. In other words, we just want to be left alone to play church and sing happy songs as the culture crumbles around us, sin ravages whole generations, and tens of millions face a godless eternity.

As I hope you have seen in the pages of this book, that retreat-and-circle-the-wagons approach is impossible to reconcile with the revealed Word—or heart—of God. Yet in many ways, *retreat* we have. I refuse to participate in retreat. At times, I wish there was not a reverse gear in my car, because as Dr. Lester Sumrall taught me, humans were created by God to go forward, not backward.

We surrendered the great universities—the historic talent pools and recruiting grounds for our nation's CEOs, ambassadors, senators, and presidents. As we saw in Chapter 7, we have abandoned vast stretches of the field of art and the humanities. The same is true to varying degrees in the realms of science, business, and media.

Some of this fatalism and defeatism is animated by a flawed understanding of the implications of Bible prophecy. Many believers today are convinced that Christ's return is imminent. I share their belief. But many have taken that confidence as a signal to give up on the culture. "Why polish the brass on a sinking ship?" they argue. Some even suggest that trying to redeem our culture is not only futile, but actually works against God's plan for the end times.

Here is the problem with this reasoning. Search the Scriptures and nowhere will you find a place in which God revokes the dominion mandate He gave the earth's first family. He commanded Adam and Eve, "Be fruitful and multiply; fill the earth and subdue it; have dominion over the fish of the sea, over the birds of the air, and over every living thing that moves on the earth" (Genesis 1:28). God gave the first two humans and their descendants specific marching orders—fill, subdue, and "have dominion."

Just prior to ascending to heaven and taking His seat at the right hand of the Father God, Jesus Christ, His Son issued an even more detailed and comprehensive dominion mandate. He said, "Go therefore and make disciples of all the nations, baptizing them in the name of the Father and of the Son and of the Holy Spirit, teaching them to observe all things that I have commanded you; and lo, I am with you always, even to the end of the age" (Matthew 28:19–20).

The church has traditionally been saying, "Come," but instead we must begin saying, "Go," as in, "Go and serve," "Go and love," "Go and give," and "Go and tell."

These are Jesus' final instructions to His disciples and to all of us who would ultimately come to follow Him because of their testimony. Did Jesus' explicit marching orders—to "make disciples of all nations" and to pass along everything He taught us—come with an expiration date? On the contrary, Christ lets us know He will be with us to help us accomplish this mission "even to the end of the age."

In fact, there are a lot of prophetic reasons to believe that those alive during the final days of history will see the most powerful and glorious moves of God ever witnessed. We are told that Jesus is returning, not for a defeated, cowering Bride, hiding from the culture behind a calloused heart, but for a glorious one without spot or wrinkle (Ephesians 5:27). And Hebrews speaks of that profoundly significant moment in which the risen, ascended Christ took His seat of authority at the right hand of the Father:

> But this Man, after He had offered one sacrifice for sins forever, sat down at the right hand of God, **from that time waiting till His enemies are made His footstool.** (Hebrews 10:12–13, emphasis added)

This passage suggests that Jesus is waiting to see something before He stands to His feet, marshals His heavenly myriads of angels, and brings history to a dramatic and predestined close. He is waiting to see His church—empowered by His Spirit, and directed by the Great Commission—walking in dominion over His enemies.

I must hasten to add, those "enemies" aren't people. "For we do not wrestle against flesh and blood, but against principalities, against powers, against the rulers of the darkness of this age, against spiritual hosts of wickedness in the heavenly places" (Ephesians 6:12). Our goal is not to subjugate our unbelieving neighbors, but rather to liberate them from the true enemies of Christ—the demonically inspired false worldviews and idolatries of this age. The enemies of Christ are also despair, family disintegration, racial hatred, disease, and lack. These are the adversaries that the church must arouse herself from slumbering lethargy and fight.

We are Jesus' feet on this earth. And it is time to win for Christ that footstool for which He continues to wait. I don't listen to a lot of contemporary music, but there are times when some of it gets my attention. One group, known as Casting Crowns, released the song *If We*

Are The Body that questions succinctly why we are not truly acting like His body.

Victory will not come if we remain sheltered behind the four walls of the sanctuary. We must be prepared to confront false worldviews in every sphere of human activity, and make a compelling argument for the truth of our biblical view.

Just what are those spheres of activity? I really like the way the organization Youth With A Mission (YWAM) breaks it out for the thousands of young people it trains each year to be effective witnesses for Christ and powerful advocates of a Christian worldview. YWAM founder Loren Cunningham has identified seven areas that must experience the redemptive influence of God's people if we are to see true cultural renewal. They are:

The Home
Religion
Schools & Education
The Media
The Arts, Entertainment, & Sports
Commerce, Science, and Technology
Government & Politics[1]

Upon reading that list, you no doubt noticed that I have already spoken directly to each of these areas to one degree or another in previous chapters. I have exposed the false worldviews that dominate the thinking of so many in these realms of activity. And we have explored the disturbing implications if we fail to spark a new Great Awakening that not only touches, but transforms each sphere.

People of faith have historically been involved and engaged in every one of these spheres, and as long as their influence was felt, the salt and light Jesus spoke of was having its intended effect. However, because the church has retreated behind its "sanctuary" walls and refused to take its rightful place in every aspect of our culture, we have not gained enemy-held territory as we have been commissioned to do. Instead, we have been polishing our armor, admiring our crowns and congratulating one another on past successes while losing a generation and a culture.

Now, I want to bring forward some additional insights that may help you understand how we must proceed if we are to prevail. These insights involve the uniquely powerful realms of politics and media.

POLITICAL ACTION IN DEFENSE OF MORAL VALUES

I begin this section on political activity well aware that there has been a tendency in the church to gravitate to one of two extremes on this matter.

It's not unusual for Christians to consider political activism a panacea that will usher in the kingdom of God if only we can get enough believers to the polls and writing enough letters to Congress. At the other end of the continuum, some sincere saints consider any focus on elections or public policy debates to be at best a waste of time and at worst a carnal and unspiritual entanglement with "the world."

Ironically, many zealous Christians have started out in the first group, but following a few of the bitter disappointments and frustrations that naturally come with trying to effect change through the ballot box, they end up in the second group.

This all-or-nothing view of engagement with the political realm is unfortunate. The truth is, political activity is important—vitally so. But it is not *all-important*. It is only one sphere of influence among the seven mentioned above.

Nevertheless, we must recognize that God has placed the American church in a representative democracy. That puts the apostle Paul's command that we submit to governmental authorities in a unique light. You see, the Christians gathering in the young churches springing up throughout the Roman provinces in the first century had no say in their government. What Caesar decreed was law. The people could only pray for just and fair treatment.

But in our nation, the people are the government. Our laws and policies directly reflect the desires and character of those who bother to participate in the process. That is why it constitutes such a tragedy when many Christians don't bother or when they participate without a thoroughly biblical worldview.

Former President James Garfield had this truth in mind when, more than 135 years ago, he wrote, "Now more than ever the people are responsible for the character of their Congress. If that body be ignorant, reckless, and corrupt, it is because the people tolerate ignorance, recklessness, and corruption. If it be intelligent, brave, and pure, it is because the people demand these high qualities to represent them in the national legislature."[2]

As has been abundantly demonstrated recently, no organization or political party has a monopoly on loose morals, bad behavior or questionable character. Poor judgment and corruption cross all political and ideological barriers, and people of faith and goodwill need to keep themselves unentangled from any association that would constrain them from speaking the truth to those to their right or left.

What does a balanced engagement in the political process look like for a Christian? There are a number of simple but significant things every believer can do to have maximum positive impact on our society. The first is the most obvious:

1. Vote, and bring a thoroughly biblical worldview with you into the voting booth. Many Christians who do vote do so only every four years—during the presidential election cycle, or at most, every two years during the mid-term elections when Congressional representatives and one-third of U.S. Senators are elected. This is a good start, but the fact is, every election is important. The outcome of races for offices such as school board, city council, mayor, and zoning board can have a significant impact on the moral climate in your city and your church's ability to minister to the community.

For example, city councils or zoning boards often must decide if and where pornography-related or "adult" entertainment establishments may be located. And many fast-growing churches have come up against resistance from city governments when it is time to buy property and build new facilities.

Furthermore, turnout for these local elections tends to be very low. This means that a handful of informed believers can have a large impact on a race.

There are many fine books and studies available that can help you formulate a biblical grid for evaluating political issues—including the ones I have cited throughout these pages. But frankly, if all you did was read this book and my previous one, *Silent No More*, you would be well ahead of most believers in this regard.

2. Understand the role of political involvement in creating moral reform. As I noted in Chapter 8: "The Battleground of the Public Square," the question before us is not *whether* religious values and paradigms will inform our laws and court rulings—but rather *whose* values and paradigm will be present at the table. The worldviews held by elected officials will guide them as they make our laws and interpret them.

We have seen that humanism, naturalism, statism, and New Age mysticism are all religious in nature. And they have been applied legislatively and legally in recent decades with disastrous moral results. The degree to which we have thus far been able to hold back the tide of moral decay is a reflection of our marginal success in electing men and women who hold a biblical worldview.

Going forward, our progress in addressing the moral tragedies of partial birth abortion, embryonic stem cell research, child pornography, and attempts to redefine the very meaning of marriage and family will be a direct reflection of how successful we are at influencing our fellow citizens. And how well we wield our influence will inevitably affect the outcome of elections. The inescapable fact is, for the Christian who cares about moral sanity in our nation, elections matter a great deal.

We got a compelling reminder of that in mid-2005 and early 2006 as

President George W. Bush had the opportunity to nominate not one but two justices to the U.S. Supreme Court, including one chief justice. Time will tell, but every indication is that Chief Justice John Roberts and Associate Justice Samuel Alito will join Justices Clarence Thomas and Antonin Scalia as voices for judicial restraint on the Court.

If George W. Bush had lost either of the last two ultra-close presidential elections, a very different type of judge would have been seated in those vacancies. We would almost certainly have gotten two more in the mold of Clinton-appointee Ruth Bader Ginsberg—a longtime active member of the American Civil Liberties Union.

And even with a Bush presidency, if there had not been a clear majority of people in the Senate, both Republicans and Democrats, who were oriented toward biblical morality, these two nominations may have suffered the same fate as did President Reagan's nomination of Robert Bork.

In Judge Bork, we could have had one of the greatest legal minds of the twentieth century on the Court, but the composition of the Senate prevented it. In his place, President Reagan nominated Anthony Kennedy. For advocates of judicial restraint, strict interpretation of the Constitution, and traditional moral values, Kennedy has been a significant disappointment. He has cast key votes with the liberal majority in several landmark cases with moral implications.

Kennedy wrote the Court's decision in *ACLU v. Ashcroft*, which had the effect of killing the Child Online Protection Act—legislation designed to enable prosecution of commercial porn sites that knowingly distribute pornography to minors. He also authored the Court's opinion in *Gonzales v. Oregon*, which ruled the U.S. attorney general could not enforce the Controlled Substances Act's provisions against physicians prescribing drugs for assisted suicide.

In 1996 Kennedy voted with the majority in *Romer v. Evans* wherein the Court overturned a voter-approved provision of the Colorado constitution that denied special group rights on the basis of sexual orientation. The *Evans* decision has been used to invalidate the efforts of other states and cities to keep "sexual orientation" out of their nondiscrimination policies. In 2003, Kennedy ruled with the majority in *Lawrence v. Texas* where the Court struck down laws against sodomy across the United States.

Here is an assessment delivered in the left-leaning Washington Post:

> . . . over the years he has repeatedly disappointed conservatives, perhaps most notably in the 1992 Planned Parenthood v. Casey ruling that upheld the constitutional right to an abortion.[3]

And as Bruce Fein observed in a Washington Times editorial decrying the way some Supreme Court justices have used bizarre sources for their rulings:

> The [1965 Griswold decision] caper spawned Supreme Court decrees inventing an unlimited constitutional right to an abortion. The court made no attempt to demonstrate either the original meaning of the Constitution or its amendments justified its extravagant holdings, for instance, that fathers have no greater interests in abortion decisions than the government. Instead, Justices Anthony Kennedy, David Souter, and O'Connor took guidance in Planned Parenthood v. Casey (1992) from "mysteries of the universe" and "the meaning of human existence."[4]

Finally, Justice Kennedy has sparked considerable dismay by actually citing *European* and *international* law in his reasoning in certain cases. (That was why you heard numerous questions posed by conservative senators to nominees Roberts and Alito during the Judiciary Committee hearings regarding whether or not they would refer to international law in deciding cases before the Court.)

In short, Kennedy's replacement of Bork has been a disaster. How different the moral, legislative, and legal landscape of our nation would be today if there had been, in both political parties, enough morally consistent and clear headed senators back in 1987 to confirm the deserving and eminently qualified Robert Bork to a seat on the highest court in the land!

Do elections matter? They matter immensely. And their outcomes have long-lasting effects.

3. Organize voter registration campaigns. In the current political context, elections are often determined purely by turnout. That was certainly the case here in my home state of Ohio in 2004 when a high turnout by traditional values voters handed the state's pivotal Electoral College votes to President Bush. If Ohio had gone the other direction, John Kerry likely would have been elected president. That's why registration drives and get-out-the-vote efforts can have a decisive effect on an election. It doesn't take any special skills or knowledge to help make sure your friends and fellow church members are registered to vote, informed about the positions of the candidates, and present at the polls on election day.

4. Practice open and constructive communication with public officials. One of the great things about living in a representative democracy is that elected officials tend to care what you think—or at least pretend to! I remember the astonishment that overcame many pastors whom I hosted for their first trip to Washington, D.C. It was difficult for them to imagine that their elected representatives would actually take time to talk to them! Nevertheless, policy makers such as legislators and city council members tend to hear most often from people who have very strong opinions about the issues under consideration. That means that a hefty percentage of the communication they receive is angry, threatening, accusatory, or just downright unpleasant. Unfortunately, that is true of some of the input they receive from people of faith and values as well.

It is, indeed, vital that our public officials hear from us. But that communication needs to be respectful, concise, and well-reasoned. Here are a few practical tips for communicating effectively with your representatives:

- Make sure your letter is addressed correctly, and check all spelling. Always do a draft first, and try to send a typed letter—it will be easier to read.
- Be brief. Write or call about one issue or bill at a time, and always identify the bill by number and/or title. A one-page letter is usually the most effective.
- Identify yourself, especially if you are a constituent.
- State your reasons for writing or calling—that you want him or her to support or oppose the bill and why. State how it will affect the legislator's district. Include or mention any relevant editorials or articles that support your position.
- Try to personalize your appeal. State your views in your words; they carry much more weight than a form letter.
- Make sure your letter or call is timely. Write or call your legislator while the issue is current and before the bill comes to the floor for debate or a vote.
- Don't forget thank-you letters and calls. Let your legislators know that you appreciate their work. A letter or call of thanks, or a compliment, will be appreciated and remembered.

When possible, cultivate personal relationships with your public officials. Find ways to serve them and minister life to them, keeping in mind the biblical principle of leadership and influence through humble servanthood.

5. Begin to build bridges between white and black Christians. Christians, black and white, obviously share a common redemption that has merged them into the same family as joint heirs with Jesus Christ. They are part of a spiritual body in which "there is neither Jew nor Greek, there is neither slave nor free, there is neither male nor female; for you are all one in Christ Jesus" (Galatians 3:28).

But many astute observers have also noted that, though they share a deep well of common values, they rarely stand united in applying political influence in advancement of those shared values. That cannot continue. Our nation cannot afford it. (See my chapter titled "Race: Fulfilling Our Fathers' Dream" in *Silent No More*.)

Many older black believers remember, with justified pain, the indifference or open resistance many white Christian churches and denominations exhibited during the important civil rights struggles in the 1960s. And many younger white Christians are puzzled and disappointed by the failure of many theologically conservative African-American saints to translate the implications of their faith and values in the voting booth.

Nevertheless, on a wide range of issues—from preservation of traditional families and marriages, to protection of the unborn, to concerns about crime and drug abuse, to a support for the global war against radical Islamic extremism—Christians of all colors stand on common ground.

In the election of 2004, President Bush made significant inroads in winning the support of African-American believers—due in some measure to the prominence of gay marriage initiatives on the ballots of several states. Yet much work remains to be done. And the heavy lifting will not be done by national political parties or large organizations. The real work of racial reconciliation among black and white Christians will happen at the individual and church levels. In other words, it is up to you and me.

People often ask me how I managed to build a church with the kind of racial balance that World Harvest Church exhibits. My answer is always the same—I never set out to make sure there were a certain number of people of any color or ethnicity in our church. We simply present the gospel, and believe that it speaks clearly to all people.

Many years ago, a local newspaper featured a different church every week. Sure enough, a reporter turned up in one of our Sunday morning meetings. He was surprised to see people ". . . in their 40s and 50s (some older) . . . [some] . . . in their 20s and 30s—black and white. A few . . . took off their shoes and danced in their happy, stockinged feet."[5]

More recently, some battle-hardened veterans of the national mainstream media told me that they had never seen such racial harmony in a church as they experienced when they paid us a visit on a Sunday morning.

During any meeting or event sponsored by our congregation, you can't look very far in any direction without seeing someone from a different background, a different nation, or whose skin is a different color. It reminds me of heaven, because the Bible says that every people group on earth will be represented before the throne of God.

I am sorry to report that most churches don't look like this. Sunday morning at 10 am is still the most racially segregated hour in America, and I maintain that racism will continue to be a stronghold in this nation until local churches and the individuals in them assume the role of leadership in its necessary demise. As Christians of all races, we need to remember that there is more that unites us than there ever could be that divides us. The greatest number of people focused on the smallest point of agreement will yield the greatest result.

MEDIA ENGAGEMENT IN PURSUIT OF CULTURAL RENEWAL

At the outset of this chapter, I pointed out that the church's default strategy when faced with cultural battle has essentially been to withdraw, retreat, and throw rocks from a safe distance. In no sphere of influence has this been more the case than in the realm of media and entertainment. And as with our withdrawals from other spheres of influence, our culture has paid a high price for our absence.

Chuck Colson has written: "The call to redeem popular culture is surely one of the most difficult challenges Christians face today. For, thanks to modern communications technology, popular culture has become intrusively pervasive . . . Popular culture is everywhere, shaping our tastes, our language, our values."[6]

But redeem it we must, if we are to fulfill the dominion mandate of the Great Commission.

In Chapter 7, "The Battleground of the Arts," I pointed out that there already exists a small but important vanguard of Christians working in Hollywood in film and television; and in the major news bureaus of New York and Washington, D.C.. This is an encouraging start, but their tribe must increase. It is a beginning made possible because men like Dr. Oral Roberts and Pat Robertson had the vision twenty years ago to create world-class media and journalism departments at places like Oral Roberts University and Regent University.

Today you will find hundreds of talented and hardworking graduates of these schools and others like them working as writers, producers, researchers, cinematographers, editors, reporters, and yes, even actors. As they have worked their way up through the ranks of their profession, they have been positioned by God to be a force for truth and cultural renewal.

Today, scores of other Christian colleges are doing the vital dual work of instilling a biblical worldview and equipping talented young believers for media excellence. To cite just one example, Biola University in Southern California offers an undergraduate degree in film/television/radio.

One Biola graduate, Scott Derrickson, recently directed the successful Hollywood film *The Exorcism of Emily Rose*, based on the true story of a German woman named Anneliese Michel, who died during an exorcism in 1976. Part supernatural thriller, part courtroom drama— *Emily Rose* was extremely popular with secular horror movie audiences even though it contained almost no blood or gore. (Note: This film is definitely not for everyone, nor is it family fare.)

Derrickson represents a needed generation of believers who choose to live and work right in the middle of the unredeemed, confused people we are supposed to influence, persuade and serve rather than isolating ourselves in a safe Christian enclave. For too long, the church has carried the flawed view that if you work at a secular job, you're not doing *ministry*. Many sold-out, Christ-loving believers have bought in to the myth that if you want to *really* serve God, you need to find a way to quit your job and go into full-time ministry.

After all, if you can't sing, play the piano or preach, what could you possibly do to serve God?

Child of God, your secular job *is* a full-time ministry! You are a subject of the King and everything to which you put your hand becomes an extension of the kingdom. We have people who are supposed to be CEOs and entrepreneurs and engineers and coaches quitting their jobs because they've been told real ministry happens only within the walls of the church. We must begin to understand the difference between "church" and the kingdom of God. All the kingdoms of this world shall "become the kingdoms of our Lord and of His Christ" (Revelation 11:15).

Every sphere of life, including that of media and entertainment, must experience the healing, redeeming touch of God's anointed people.

There are two aspects to the Great Commission. First, we must win the lost by preaching the Gospel. Next, we must make disciples of those we have won, thereby reshaping the culture in which we live.

We must advance, not retreat. We must engage, not withdraw. Believers can and should operate at a high level of excellence in every sphere of society. We are in His Majesty's Special Service. Thus, we must begin to think like loyal subjects of the King.

ACTION POINTS

- Be an informed voter and encourage like-minded friends to be the same. This is important not only for "big" elections like the presidential races but for local offices and ballot initiatives.
- Get involved in the political process by attending party caucuses and precinct meetings as well as supporting good candidates with your time, finances and influence.
- Vote for U.S. Senators who will pledge to confirm only federal judges who adhere to a philosophy of judicial restraint and who will oppose activist judges. Vote for presidential candidates who will nominate such judges.
- With appropriate permission, organize a voter registration campaign in your church or civic organization.
- Let your representatives hear from you, but always be respectful, well-reasoned and non-personal. Persuade, don't threaten.
- Let racial reconciliation begin with you. Reach out to a person of another race and cultivate a friendship.
- Suggested reading:

Can a Christian Influence Politics?: How to Make a Difference in Government, by Roy Herron.[7]
Living in Color: Embracing God's Passion for Ethnic Diversity, by Randy Woodley.[8]
Winning the Race to Unity: Is Racial Reconciliation Really Working?, by Clarence Shuler.[9]

twelve

A SEED, A GENERATION

They have come to be known as *the Greatest Generation.*

Tom Brokaw used the term in his book of the same name to describe the amazing courage, character, and selfless spirit of the generation that was just coming of age at the outbreak of World War II. The name stuck and has now become part of the cultural vocabulary of our nation. Brokaw opens *The Greatest Generation* with these words:

> When the United States entered World War II, the U.S. government turned to ordinary Americans and asked of them extraordinary service, sacrifice and heroics.[1]

As we know, they were equal to the challenge. And because they were, we are in their debt. And we stand on their broad shoulders.

Today, if you'll listen with your spirit, you'll hear our Savior asking something very similar of us. And America, though in a different kind of jeopardy than that presented by the Axis powers in 1941, needs us just as desperately.

In the film *Saving Private Ryan*, a classic treatment of the sacrifices associated with war, many men put their lives on the line to save one. This kind of sacrifice has always been recognized as heroic, but necessary in times of grave danger or national crisis. We honor those who served in World War II and build memorials to recognize the value of what they were willing to do—and well we should.

Today, God is looking for a few who will stand in the gap to save many—a saving remnant. He's seeking a people who take seriously the Bible's call to "lay aside every weight, and the sin which so easily ensnares us" so that we might "run with endurance the race that is set before us, looking unto Jesus, the author and finisher of our faith, who for the joy that was set before Him endured the cross, despising the shame, and has sat down at the right hand of the throne of God." (Hebrews 12:1, 2)

God is looking for His "greatest generation", and He has focused His gaze upon us. You see, God knows that if He gets the seed, He gets the whole harvest, but only if that seed is willing to die. I know that sounds cryptic. Allow me to explain.

Buried in Psalm 22 is a difficult verse. It is one I suspect most people just read right past without comprehending the amazing promise it contains:

> A seed shall serve him; it shall be accounted to the Lord for a generation. (v. 30 KJV)

The Word of God here is using an agricultural metaphor. In a sack of seeds resides the potential for an entire harvest. And in biblical times, once a harvest of grain was brought in, a wise farmer would set aside a portion of that harvest as seed for the next one. Even in more recent days, before hybridization became commonplace, farmers would hold back the best of their harvest to be used as next year's seed.

When times were hard in the hills of Kentucky, my mother remembers that as a little girl she heard serious discussions about seed corn that was carefully selected and saved. In the long nights and short days of late winter, just about anything was used as table fare to feed a hungry family, but the seed corn was sacrosanct. Without seed, there would be no harvest next year, and that seed was protected and preserved until it could be planted. It literally meant the difference between sufficiency and starvation for an entire family.

So, in farming terms, a *seed* is the set-apart portion of a *harvest*. If no seed was saved, no harvest would be forthcoming.

Of course, God makes it clear in Psalm 22:30 that He is not making a point about farming. The second half of the verse lets us know He is referring to *people*—"a generation."

Here is what I believe God is saying to us through this verse: "If I can get the seed, I can get the whole generation." I am convinced that we, God's people, are the seed for the current generation of Americans. I am talking about delivering to God a purchased generation!

Here is the problem. For seed to produce, it must die. This is precisely what Jesus tells us in John 12:24: "Most assuredly, I say to you, unless a grain of wheat falls into the ground and dies, it remains alone; but if it dies, it produces much grain." But as with Psalm 22:30, Jesus isn't offering farming tips. He is speaking symbolically of people—you and me. He makes that clear in the very next verse:

> He who loves his life will lose it, and he who hates his life in this world
> will keep it for eternal life. (John 12:25)

Our heavenly Father is looking for a remnant of believers today who are willing to be the seed for this generation. If He can find a seed willing to make a sacrifice for their peers, He will reap a harvest of an entire generation, and we will see the transforming power of God at work in every area of our culture. God gave us the perfect example by sending His Son, Jesus Christ, as the ultimate sacrifice for all of us. In a similar way, we are that seed for our generation. But we have not "been accounted to the Lord for a generation," because, very simply, we have refused to die.

As I have mentioned with sorrow several times on the pages of this book, the church in our nation is, on the whole, self-absorbed, pleasure-driven, and comfort-seeking. Obsessed with entertainment and yet utterly bored, we are in the midst of what author Neil Postman has described as "amusing ourselves to death."[2] Convenience, not commitment, has become paramount. Self-help books fly out of retailers' displays and become best-sellers, while those that require self-examination or even careful thought gather dust on the shelves. You don't sell many books with themes such as, "How to be crucified with Christ." We have an insatiable appetite for "self-help," and little stomach for self-denial.

Since it was the apostle Paul who coined the phrase "crucified with Christ," let me take that thought a little further using him as an example. Suppose that a young man who felt called to carry the message of Jesus Christ came to the great apostle and said he wanted to learn from him how to develop the same kind of faith and determination to preach the gospel to the nations. He asked Paul to pray for him.

"You want the same kind of determination that I have? You want to develop your faith to enable you to reach the nations? Certainly, I will pray for you."

The young man lowered his head to receive what he thought would surely be the veteran preacher's blessing and benediction.

"Lord," Paul began, "this young man desires the faith that resides in my heart. He wants to see mountains move. He wants to preach to the nations."

"This is it," the young man thought. "Now I'm going to receive what I desire most." He could almost see himself ministering to the multitudes, confounding the wise and having a name that was known throughout the world.

"Lord," Paul continued, "let him be beaten. Let him be stoned. Let him be persecuted by those who hate him without cause."

"Uh, Paul?" the young man said.

"I'm not finished. Lord, let him be shipwrecked, let him be given up for dead, let him be a traveler who seldom sees his home or his family . . ."

"I don't think . . ."

"Don't interrupt me. Lord, let him be in peril in floods, and from brigands, and let him be betrayed by those who call themselves his friends . . ."

"But that's not what I . . ."

"Hold on, my boy. You said you wanted what I had, and I want you to know how I got it. Lord, let him be in peril among the heathen, and in the city, and in the wilderness; let him be weary, let him be awake all night when everyone else is asleep, let him be hungry and thirsty, and cold and at risk of exposure to the elements . . ."

But by this time, the young man who said he wanted Paul's faith was long gone.

Of course, not everyone is destined to go through what the apostle Paul had to endure in order to finish his course. But we will inevitably have to encounter some kind of adversity if we are to reverse the moral decline in our generation, and we have become so adept at avoiding this that many people think that living a life pleasing to God means little more than living a life that is pleasing to them.

We have asked and answered the question, "What's in it for me?" so often that we have forgotten it's not really about us at all. Even our best presentations of salvation focus on what we want. "Come to Jesus," we say, "because He has a wonderful plan for your life." No wonder those who do listen and respond remain self-centered and essentially indistinguishable from those who do not—they are deceived and believe that they will gain everything and be required to give up nothing.

There is no doubt that God has a wonderful plan for your life and mine, but that plan involves making some sacrifices. This is a part of being an example to a generation, but is a detail many have either chosen to ignore or have eliminated altogether. We must accept all of God's will for us, not just those portions that happen to appeal and bring instant gratification and pleasure to us. That is secular human-ism, not biblical Christianity. Instead of desiring the whole grain bread of life, which is unattractive but has nutritive value, we have been seeking cotton candy, artificially colored and whipped up with hot air, with enough sweetness to temporarily satisfy our appetites but with no substance to sustain our lives.

We have presented a gospel that is essentially escapism. We invite people to come into a "sanctuary" as though we are offering a place where they can hide from all the evil negative influences and uncertainty that surrounds them. All the while, God's desire and plan is for a people who will confidently step outside those pseudo-religious walls and invade the darkness of our culture—shining representatives of the Light of the World—illuminating the path that leads to the redeeming love of Christ for hurting humanity.

Far too often, sadly, in many instances, we have turned the training ground of the church into a sanctified success seminar wherein the glorious truths and precious promises of the Bible are manipulatively and selectively employed as tools for getting everything we think we want. We live in bigger houses, drive faster cars, wear designer clothes, and eat finer food, but remain empty because we fail to fulfill our God-given purpose.

Who can forget the images of the first responders on 9-11 rushing into burning buildings that were in danger of collapse while others were rushing out? All the advanced equipment and technology in the world could not substitute for the courage they displayed in the face of danger. As a result, they are rightly regarded as heroes. But how would we have felt about them if they had not answered when the bell rang at their station? We would have criticized them as derelict in their duty, or called them cowards, or worse.

How, then, should we see ourselves in the light of truth when the call for rescue goes out, and those who have the means to throw a lifeline to a godless and faithless generation continue to polish their expensive equipment, but utterly fail to put it to its intended use?

Many pastors have measured their success on the basis of how many people they have *coming* to their services, instead of how many people they have *going* . . . into all the world making disciples.

Jesus warned people that to follow Him called for some serious cost-counting. He warned people not to make the decision to follow

Him in a cavalier fashion. Yet the contemporary American church has applied so much "marketing" savvy to the gospel, an entire generation of believers has been led to believe that following Christ would lead to a life free from struggle or opposition in this world, in addition to a home in heaven for eternity.

Here lies the paradox of the *real* gospel. A correct interpretation of Scripture necessarily leads to the biblical truth that the only way to experience true happiness is to die to self-will. When Jesus told His disciples to follow Him, they all understood that would mean leaving their own plans, purposes, and pursuits. We must recapture that same understanding.

And a seed shall serve Him, and it shall be counted unto Him for a generation. It is very simple. If we give ourselves to God as a seed, if we present ourselves to Him—sold out, fully surrendered, He will receive our generation as a harvest!

What is necessary for us to become that seed that is available to God? It will require the bravery and strength to follow the example of Jesus as He cringed under the full light of a Passover moon in an olive grove called Gethsemane, just across the Kidron Valley from the ancient city of Jerusalem. He was there to be prepared as the ultimate sacrifice. He was there to become sure that He was willing to die. Otherwise, Calvary would be no more than a crime scene and the Son of God no more than a murder victim—God would forever be a liar and sin would rule the crazed hearts of men for eternity.

Hear Him hurl an agonized cry to the heavens, and mark His example well, for this was where victory over death and its cruel companions, hell and the grave, was won. Hear Him as He says the words that come not from a casual acquaintance with God, but from a heart full of assurance of the character of His heavenly Father, who promised success on the other side of a borrowed tomb—this is what Christ's cry was on that lonely evening long ago—"Not my will, but Yours be done." Our culture will continue its downward spiral until we echo that cry.

WHY WE ARE HERE

In Chapter 10 I described your God-given call and purpose on the earth as being "to place the jewel of a soul in the crown of our Savior— that the Lamb of God slain may receive the reward of His suffering."

Those words, "the reward of His suffering," are not mine. It is an old phrase carried all over the world on the lips of a people known as the Moravians.

The Moravian Christians were a persecuted Protestant minority in Central Europe before there was any such thing as a Protestant. One hundred years before Martin Luther, the Moravians rejected many of the abuses and errors of Rome and pursued a simple faith of worship and charity. As a result, they were severely persecuted, and they suffered great hardship.

Nevertheless, they are marked by history for their extraordinary compassion, their service, and above all, their passion for souls.

In the early 1700s, Moravians began coming to the New World. Some came because they were escaping persecution or because they were being forced from their homes. Others were compelled by a powerful missionary impulse. For example, some saw the swelling population of slaves being transported to the colonies in the Americas and wondered how these poor souls might be reached for Christ.

The treatment of slaves everywhere in the New World was appalling, but in the West Indies it was especially so. The seemingly endless supply of fresh slaves available from Africa convinced Caribbean plantation owners that they didn't need to provide any care for their slaves at all. They literally worked them to death and ordered replacements. It was this group of shackled and shamed humanity that the Moravians desired to reach. But how?

Their solution was to sell themselves into slavery. The only way to reach the slaves was to become one of them. They were aware that such a decision would result in ridicule, in harsh conditions and even harsher treatment, and could mean death. Yet they did so with willing hearts.

On October 8, 1732, a Dutch ship left Copenhagen harbor bound for the Danish West Indies. On board were two Moravian missionaries: John Leonard Dober, a potter; and David Nitschman, a carpenter. Both were on their way to sell themselves into slavery to reach the slaves of the West Indies.

As the ship slipped away, they looked to their friends and loved ones at the dock and lifted up a cry that would ring in the ears of future generations of Moravian missionaries, "May the Lamb that was slain receive the reward of His suffering!"

Some historians estimate that eighty thousand slaves came to a saving knowledge of Jesus Christ through the efforts of Moravian missionaries. They were seeds, willing to fall into the ground and die, that their King might receive the harvest of a generation. They understood what many of us do not. We are placed on this earth for this fleeting wisp of time not to be comfortable, but to comfort; not to be served, but to serve; to bring glory to God, not ourselves.

This is at the heart of the apostle Paul's encouragement:

Have this attitude in yourselves which was also in Christ Jesus, who, although He existed in the form of God, did not regard equality with God a thing to be [selfishly clung to], but emptied Himself, taking the form of a bond-servant, and being made in the likeness of men. And being found in appearance as a man, He humbled Himself by becoming obedient to the point of death, even death on a cross. (Philippians 2:5–8, NASB)

That is why we're here. But that is not the whole picture. The fact is, people who quit living for themselves and start living fully for Christ and the people He died to redeem, experience unspeakable blessing, joy, fulfillment, and reward—not just in heaven someday, but right now, in this life.

That is what Jesus told a group of people who were discussing all they were going to have to give up to follow Him—friends, family, jobs, wealth. Jesus' response was:

Assuredly, I say to you, there is no one who has left house or brothers or sisters or father or mother or wife or children or lands, for My sake and the gospel's, who shall not receive a hundredfold now in this time—houses and brothers and sisters and mothers and children and lands, with persecutions—and in the age to come, eternal life. (Mark 10:29–30)

That is why we're here. "This is the generation of those who seek Him, / Who seek Your face" (Psalm 24:6 NASB). Let us become the generation that seeks God's face fully and unreservedly. Let us be God's greatest generation.

OUR WAR OF THE WORLDS

I opened this volume with a call to battle. My hope is that I have articulated that call clearly and compellingly, because much is at stake. You see, when worldviews collide, nations hang in the balance.

As I have stated, we are currently experiencing a full-scale, multi-pronged cultural offensive aimed at removing, once and for all, traditional faith and morality from our laws, courts, schools, and marketplaces. World War II asked of that generation "extraordinary service, sacrifice and heroics." This current "war of the worlds" demands no less.

As with the Battle of the Bulge, all the gains we have made in recent years are in danger of being wiped out in a sudden and ferocious counterattack by the forces of secularism and humanism. In the process, the God-given disciplines of science and the arts are being misused as weapons in this cultural conflict for the hearts of our fellow citizens.

As with the Jewish resistance in Israel under the Greeks, we are under intense pressure to surrender our distinctiveness and allow ourselves to be assimilated into the idolatrous, pagan popular culture.

The culture isn't demanding that we sacrifice a pig on a holy altar.

The culture demands something even more profane—that we sacrifice the truth of the gospel on the altar of political and cultural correctness. They want us to stop proclaiming that Jesus is the only way of salvation, or that He is the Way, the Truth, and the Life—and that no one comes to the Father except through Him.

There is a price we must pay to save a generation, restore a nation, and revitalize a civilization. The question is, are we willing to pay that price? The Commander of the hosts of heaven is standing by to grace our efforts and assure us of victory—if only we will summon the courage to fight. I don't know about you, but I was built for the battle and created for the conflict and I don't want to march in a parade. I want to be in a battle. I don't want to lead a marching band. I want to lead an army!

Let us love our lost and floundering neighbors enough to tell them the truth. In a spirit of humility and compassion, let us confront them with the moral and spiritual bankruptcy of their worldviews. I say to the church what Jesus said in his prophetic message to the church in Sardis in Revelation 3:2 (NIV): "Wake up! Strengthen what remains and is about to die."

Wake up, we must. So I will summon my brothers and sisters to battle. For when worldviews collide, nations hang in the balance.

ACTION POINTS

- Become a seed, willing to die to self-will. That means laying down your life, your comfort, your own agenda and truly becoming a disciple of Christ. Determine to become a part of God's "greatest generation."
- Ask God to make your life count utmost. Ask Him for the courage and strength to do whatever he calls you to do in this critical moment in our nation's history.
- Read about the history of the Moravian Christians in the online book, *Behold the Lamb: The Story of the Moravian Church*, by Peter Hoover at http://allgodsword.com/Btl/.

notes

INTRODUCTION

1. David Limbaugh, *Persecution: How Liberals Are Waging War Against Christianity* (Washington, D.C.: Perennial, 2004), x.
2. Thom S. Rainer, *The Bridger Generation: America's Second Largest Generation, What They Believe, How to Reach Them* (B & H Publishing Group, Nashville, TN, June 1997).
3. WorldNetDaily, February 18, 2005.
4. Ibid.
5. Charles Colson and Nancy Pearcey, *How Now Shall We Live?* (Wheaton, Illinois: Tyndale House, 1999), x.

PART 1

1. Http://www.mm.com/user/jpk/battle.htm.

CHAPTER 1

1. Charles Dickens, *A Tale of Two Cities* (New York: Signet Classics/New American Library, 1960), 13.
2. Http://www.barna.org/FlexPage.aspx?Page=Topic&TopicID=8.
3. Steven Gertz, "Is Speaking Truth a Hate Crime?" Christianity Today online, http://www.christianitytoday.com/history/newsletter/2004/aug5.html.
4. Http://www.akegreen.org/news.htm.

5. The Christian Film and Television Commission, news release, February 6, 2006.

6. Rod Parsley, *Silent No More: Bringing Moral Clarity to America . . . While Freedom Still Rings* (Lake Mary, Florida: Charisma House, 2005), 23.

7. Benton Johnson, Dean R. Hoge, and Donald A. Luidens, "Mainline Churches: The Real Reason for Decline," *First Things* no. 31, March 1993.

8. Gloria Steinem, Essay, *Saturday Review of Education*, March 1973.

9. Paul Kurtz and Edwin H. Wilson, Humanist Manifesto II, http://www.americanhumanist.org/about/manifesto2.html. (Original signatories included science fiction writer Isaac Asimov; environmentalist Lester Brown; poet John Ciardi; Francis Crick, one of the scientists who discovered DNA; Russian scientist Andre Sakharow; psychologist B. F. Skinner; philosopher Henry Nelson Wieman; and Betty Friedan, the founder of the National Organization for Women. Since 1973, several thousand others have signed the declaration.).

10. ABC News transcripts, *World News Tonight*, January 16, 2001, http://www.transcripts.tv/search/do_details.cfm?ShowDetailID=18411.

11. Laura Blumenfeld, "Soros's Deep Pockets vs. Bush," *Washington Post*, November 11, 2003.

12. John E. O'Neill and Jerome R. Corsi, *Unfit for Command: Swift Boat Veterans Speak Out Against John Kerry* (Washington D.C.: Regnery Publishing, Inc., 2004).

13. http://www.oprah.com/tows/pastshows/200409/tows_past_20040929.html.

14. *Silent No More*, pp.xv-xvi.

15. Robert Reich, Bush's God, *The American Prospect*, http://www.prospect.org/web/page.ww?section=root&name=ViewPrint&articleId=7858.

16. *The New Yorker*, September 2004.

17. Don Feder, "Anti-Christian Fundamentalists," FrontPageMagazine.com, September 14, 2004, http://frontpagemag.org/Articles/ReadArticle.asp?ID=15081.

18. Hugh Hewitt, "The New McCarthyism, *World Magazine*, April 30, 2005.

19. WorldNetDaily, January 8, 2006, http://www.worldnetdaily.com/news/article.asp?ARTICLE_ID=48252.

20. http://www.thegodmovie.com/dvd.php.

21. Stephanie Merritt, *The Observer*, February 6, 2005.

22. Dean Hamer, *The God Gene: How Faith Is Hardwired into Our Genes* (New York: Doubleday, 2004).

23. Carl Zimmer, "Faith Boosting Genes," Scientific American, October 2004.

24. George Barna, *The Second Coming of the Church: A Blueprint for Survival* (Nashville: Word Publishing, 1998), 5.

25. George Barna, *Revolution: Finding Vibrant Faith Beyond the Walls of the Sanctuary*, (Wheaton, Illinois: BarnaBooks; 2005), 35.

26. George Barna, *The Second Coming of the Church*, op. cit.,p. 6.

27. "Abortion Common Among All Women", The Alan Guttmacher Institute, 2004, http://www.guttmacher.org/media/nr/prabort2.html.

28. George Barna, *The Second Coming of the Church*, op. cit., 6.

29. George Barna, *Revolution*, op. cit., 35.

30. Ibid., 33.

31. George Barna, *The Second Coming of the Church*, op. cit., 6.

32. Ibid., 33.

33. Ibid., 32.

34. *A Profile of Protestant Pastors in Anticipation of 'Pastor Appreciation Month'*, September 25, 2001, www.barna.org.

35. *Going Public With the Gospel* (Downers Grove, Ill.: InterVarsity Press, 2003), p. 94.

36. Nancy Pearcey, *Total Truth: Liberating Christianity From Its Cultural Captivity*, (Wheaton, Illinois: Crossway Books, 2004), 44.

37. Elisabeth Noelle-Neumann, *The Spiral of Silence: Our Social Skin*, Chicago, IL. University of Chicago Press, 2nd Ed. November 15, 1993.

38. P. Andrew Sandlin, "The Myth of the Culture Wars," WorldNetDaily Commentary, January 27, 2000, http://www.wnd.com/news/article.asp?ARTICLE_ID=16283.

39. George Barna, *Revolution*, op. cit., 32.

40. Pamela R. Winnick, *A Jealous God: Science's Crusade Against Religion*, (Nashville: Nelson Current, 2005).

41. Nancy Pearcey, *Total Truth: Liberating Christianity From Its Cultural Captivity*, (Wheaton, Illinois: Crossway Books, 2004).

42. Rod Parsley, *Silent No More: Bringing Moral Clarity to America . . . While Freedom Still Rings* (Lake Mary, Florida: Charisma House, 2005).

43. David Limbaugh, *Persecution: How Liberals Are Waging War Against Christianity* (Washington, D.C.: Perennial, 2003).

CHAPTER 2

1. Cassie Bernall was a junior at Columbine High in Littleton, Colorado. Numerous eyewitnesses report that on the day of the killings in April of 1999, several of the students who were in the library where Cassie and others were shot said she had been confronted by one of the gunmen, Dylan Klebold, and asked whether she believed in God. It was reported that she said "yes" and was immediately shot and killed. Her story became a spark for spiritual renewal among many young people around the country and resulted in a best-selling book written by her mother, Misty Bernall, titled *She Said "Yes."*

2. G. K. Chesterton, *Heretics*, in *The Complete Works of G. K. Chesterton*, ed. David Dooley, vol. 1 (San Francisco: Ignatius Press, 1986), 41.

3. Charles Colson, Foreword, in *Making the Connections: How to Put Biblical Worldview Integration into Practice*; Christian Overman; (Puyallup, Washington: The Biblical Worldview Institute; 2003).

4. John Ward Anderson, "6 Billion and Counting—but Slower," *Washington Post,* October 12, 1999, A01, http://www.washingtonpost.com/wp-srv/inatl/feed/a46920-1999oct12.htm.

5. Ibid.

6. http://www.democraticunderground.com/discuss/duboard.php?az=show_topic&forum =103&topic_id=11132.

7. James W. Sire, *The Universe Next Door*, 4th ed. (Downers Grove, Illinois: InterVarsity Press, 2004), 17.

8. David Noebel, *Understanding the Times: The Religious Worldviews of Our Day and the Search for Truth* (Eugene, Oregon; Harvest House, 1991), 1.

9. James W. Sire, *The Universe Next Door*, op. cit.

10. Francis Schaeffer, *A Christian Manifesto* (Wheaton, Illinois: Crossway Books, 1981).

11. James W. Sire, *Naming the Elephant: Worldview as a Concept*, (Downers Grove, IL: InterVarsity Press, 2004).

CHAPTER 3

1. Alvin Toffler, *Future Shock* (New York: Bantam, 1984), p. 47.

2. Sheryl Crow to reporters backstage at the 2003 American Music Awards, January 13, 2003.

3. Carl Sagan, *Cosmos* (New York: Ballantine Books, 1985), 1.

4. Peter Singer, *Practical Ethics* (New York: Cambridge University Press, 1979), 122–23.

5. http://www.americanhumanist.org/about/manifesto1.html.

6. Humanist Manifesto II, American Humanist Society, http://www.jcn.com/manifestos.html.

7. Herbert Schlossberg, *Idols for Destruction: The Conflict of Christian Faith and American Culture* (Crossway, 1990), 39.

8. Ibid

9. Paul Kurtz, "Is Everyone a Humanist?" in *The Humanist Alternative*, ed. Paul Kurtz (Buffalo: Prometheus Books, 1973), 177.

10. David Noebel, *Understanding the Times,* op. cit., 69.

11. Stephane Courtois et al., *The Black Book of Communism* (Cambridge, Massachusetts: Harvard University Press, 1999).

12. Ibid.

13. Andrew Natsios, The Politics of Famine in North Korea, United States Institute of Peace—Special Report #51, http://www.usip.org/pubs/specialreports/sr990802.html.

14. BBC News, http://news.bbc.co.uk/1/hi/talking_point/4574991.stm.

15. United States Supreme Court Justice Oliver Wendell Holmes, quoted in Richard Hertz, *Chance and Symbol* (Chicago: University of Chicago Press, 1948), 107.

16. James Sire, *The Universe Next Door* (Downers Grove, Illinois: InterVarsity Press, 2004), 64.

17. Dean Hamer, *The God Gene* (New York: Doubleday, 2004).

18. http://en.wikipedia.org/wiki/Louis_B._Mayer.

19. *Getting to Know "Connected Mathematics Project"* (1996), Teacher's Guide, 17.

20. Nancy Pearcey, *Total Truth: Liberating Christianity from Its Cultural Captivity* (Wheaton, Illinois: Crossway Books, 2004), 44.

21. *The American Heritage® Dictionary of the English Language*, 4th ed. (Boston: Houghton Mifflin Company, 2000).

22. Of course, as with most violent celebrity deaths, alternative conspiracy theories abound on the Internet.

23. Charles Colson, Nancy Pearcy, & Harold Fickett, *How Now Shall We Live?* (Tyndale House Publishers, 1999).

24. Douglas Groothuis, *Truth Decay: Defending Christianity Against the Challenges of Postmodernism* (InterVarsity Press, 2000).

25. James W. Sire, *The Universe Next Door* (InterVarsity Press, 1997).

CHAPTER 4

1. David Noebel, *Understanding the Times: The Religious Worldviews of Our Day and the Search for Truth* (Eugene, Oregon: Harvest House, 1991).

2. Ibid.

3. Nancy Pearcey, *Total Truth: Liberating Christianity from Its Cultural Captivity* (Wheaton, Illinois: Crossway Books, 2004).

4. David Noebel, *Understanding the Times: The Religious Worldviews of Our Day and the Search for Truth* (Eugene, Oregon: Harvest House, 1991).

5. Ibid.

6. Ibid.

7. Ibid.

8. Ibid.

9. Ibid.

10. Ibid.

11. *Message* by John Ashcroft, http://www.csec.org/csec/sermon/ashcroft_3011.htm.

12. David Noebel, *Understanding the Times: The Religious Worldviews of Our Day and the Search for Truth* (Eugene, Oregon; Harvest House, 1991).

13. Herbert Schlossberg, Charles Colson & Robert H. Bork, *Idols for Destruction: The Conflict of Christian Faith and American Culture* (Wheaton Illinois: Crossway Books, 1993).

14. David Noebel, *Understanding the Times: The Religious Worldviews of Our Day and the Search for Truth* (Eugene, Oregon: Harvest House, 1991).

15. Ibid.

16. Rodney Stark, *The Victory of Reason: How Christianity Led to Freedom, Capitalism, and Western Success* (Random House, 2005).

CHAPTER 5

1. David Noebel, *Understanding the Times: The Religious Worldviews of Our Day and the Search for Truth* (Eugene, Oregon: Harvest House, 1991).

2. Ibid.

3. Ibid.

4. Ibid.

5. Ibid.

6. Ibid.

7. Ibid.

8. Ibid.

9. Ibid.

10. Ibid.

11. Ibid.

12. *Silent No More*, Ch. 6, p. 121.

13. David Noebel, *Understanding the Times: The Religious Worldviews of Our Day and the Search for Truth* (Eugene, Oregon: Harvest House, 1991).

14. Ibid.

15. Ibid.

16. Ibid.

17. Ibid.

18. *The Autobiography of Charles Darwin*, Kessinger Publishing, Whitefish, MT, 2004.

19. David Noebel, *Understanding the Times: The Religious Worldviews of Our Day and the Search for Truth* (Eugene, Oregon: Harvest House, 1991).

20. Ibid.

21. http://en.wikipedia.org/wiki/Sigmund_Freud.

22. David Noebel, *Understanding the Times: The Religious Worldviews of Our Day and the Search for Truth* (Eugene, Oregon: Harvest House, 1991).

23. Ibid.

24. Ibid.

25. Ibid.

26. Dave Breese, *Seven Men Who Rule the World from the Grave* (Chicago: Moody Press, 1990).

27. Richard Webster, *Why Freud Was Wrong* (New York: BasicBooks, 1995).

CHAPTER 6

1. Speech given on November 11, 1948. Reproduced in Omar Bradley's *Collected Writings*, vol. 1 (Washington, D.C.: Library of Congress, 1967).

2. *Wired* magazine, October 1999, "Shrink-to-Fit Genes," by Jennifer Frazier.

3. *New Scientist*, November 21, 1998, 14.

4. PBS documentary *Bloodlines,* http://www.pbs.org/bloodlines/timeline/text_ timeline.html.

5. Robert Moffitt, Ph.D., Kelly Hollowell, Ph.D., Phil Coelho, and Rep. Dave Weldon, R-FL. *Federal Stem Cell Research: What Taxpayers Should Know,* The Heritage Foundation, March 24, 2005.

6. Ibid.

7. Ibid.

8. *U.S. News & World Report,* "Mixing Species—and Crossing a Line?" by Nell Boyce, October 27, 2003.

9. *Washington Post,* November 20, 2004, "Of Mice, Men and In-Between: Scientists Debate Blending of Human, Animal Forms," by Rick Weiss.

10. Rodney Stark, *For the Glory of God: How Monotheism Led to Reformations, Science, Witch-Hunts, and the End of Slavery* (Princeton University Press, 2004), 156f.

11. Meghan Kleppenger, http://www.cwfa.org/articledisplay.asp? id=9774&department=CWA&categoryid=education.

12. Rod Parsley, *Silent No More* (Lake Mary, Florida: Charisma House, 2005), 29

13. *Silent No More,* p. 24.

14. Richard Greco Jr., speech before the White House Office of White House Fellowships, December 2, 2002.

15. Chuck Colson, *Breakpoint Commentary,* August 12, 2004, http://www.pfm.org/AM/Template.cfm?Section=BreakPoint1&template= /CM/HTMLDisplay.cfm&ContentID=16035.

16. *Silent No More,* p. 10.

17. *The Daily Telegraph,* February 26, 2006, "'Name and Shame' Tactic Stops Indians Aborting Baby Girls," by Amrit Dhillon.

18. Ibid.

19. Ibid.

20. *Boston Globe,* June 27, 2005, "Test Reveals Gender Early in Pregnancy," by Carey Goldberg.

21. *New York Times,* June 20, 2004, "A New Test for Fetal Defects, Agonizing Choices," by Amy Harmon.

22. *Silent No More,* Epilogue, p.179.

23. *Alberta Report,* April, 12, 1999, "Canadian Nurses Forced to Perform Late-Term, Genetic-Based Abortions."

24. ChristianityToday.com, "Aborting the Disabled" by Rob Moll, http://www.christianitytoday.com/ct/2005/116/42.0.html.

25. Jack Kim, Reuters, March 22, 2006, http://reuters.myway.com/article/20060322/2006-03-22T123122Z_01_SEO27580_RTRIDST_0_NEWS-KOREA-NORTH-RIGHTS-DC.html.

26. *Wired* magazine, January 1997, "Evolution Revolution" by Charles Platt.

27. Nigel Cameron as quoted by Chuck Colson, *Breakpoint Commentary*, "The Biotech Century: Dream or Nightmare?" February 27, 2006, http://www.pfm.org/AM/Template.cfm?Section=BreakPoint1&Template=/CM/ContentDisplay.cfm&ContentID=18117.

28. Rodney Stark, *For the Glory of God: How Monotheism Led to Reformations, Science, Witch-Hunts, and the End of Slavery* (Princeton University Press, 2004).

29. Leon R. Kass, M.D., *Life, Liberty, and the Defense of Dignity: The Challenge for Bioethics,* (San Francisco: Encounter Books, 2004).

30. Francis Fukuyama, *Our Posthuman Future: Consequences of the Biotechnology Revolution,* (New York: Farrar, Strauss and Giroux, 2002).

CHAPTER 7

1. *NY Arts Magazine.* February 8, 2006.

2. http://www.foxnews.com/story/0,2933,108861,00.html.

3. David Limbaugh, *Persecution: How Liberals Are Waging War Against Christianity* (Washington, D.C.: Perennial, 2003), 265.

4. Writing about such moves already underway in Canada, Kurtz stated: "The way to abolish marriage, without seeming to abolish it, is to redefine the institution out of existence. If everything can be marriage, pretty soon nothing will be marriage. Legalize gay marriage, followed by multi-partner marriage, and pretty soon the whole idea of marriage will be meaningless. At that point, Canada can move to what Bailey and her friends really want: an infinitely flexible relationship system that validates any conceivable family arrangement, regardless of the number or gender of partners." (National Review Online, Stanley Kurtz's "Dissolving Marriage: If Everything Is Marriage, Then Nothing Is," February 3, 2006, http://www.nationalreview.com/kurtz/kurtz200602030805.asp.).

5. *The Atlantic,* December 2005, "Can Jesus Save Hollywood?" by Hanna Rosin.

6. NPR's *Morning Edition*, August 1, 2001.

7. Francis A. Schaeffer, *How Should We Then Live?*, Chapter 4.

8. http://www.QuotationsBook.com/quotes/Al_Capp.

9. Ravi Zacharias, Address to the United Nations' Prayer Breakfast, September 10, 2002, Ravi Zacharias International Ministries, http://www.rzim.org/publications/essay_arttext.php?id=13.

10. David Limbaugh, *Persecution,* op. cit., 267.

11. Nancy Pearcey, *Total Truth: Liberating Christianity from Its Cultural Captivity,* (Crossway Books, 2004), 57.

12. Francis A. Schaeffer, *Art and the Bible,* Chapter 1.

13. Francis A. Schaeffer, *Art and the Bible,* (Downers Grove, IL: Intervarsity Press, 1973).

14. Laura Ingraham, *Shut Up and Sing: How Elites from Hollywood, Politics, and the UN are Subverting America,* (Regnery Publishing, 2003).

15. Shane Hipps, *The Hidden Power of Electronic Culture: How Media Shapes Faith, the Gospel and the Church* (Zondervan, 2006).

16. Bernard Goldberg, Bias: A CBS Insider Exposes How the Media Distorts the News, (Washington, D.C.: Regnery, 2002).

CHAPTER 8

1. *Silent No More*, p. 2.

2. Maureen Dowd, as cited by TimesWatch.org, http://www.timeswatch.org/articles/2004/1116.asp#2.

3. Mary Ann Glendon, "The Women of Roe v. Wade," *First Things,* June/July 2003, http://www.firstthings.com/ftissues/ft0306/articles/glendon.html.

4. Luther's Works, Weimar Edition, *Briefwechsel* [Correspondence], vol. 3, p. 81.

5. Joseph Loconte and Jennifer Marshall, "Religious Hiring Protection Under Assault," Web Memo #413, February 3, 2004, the Heritage Foundation, http://www.heritage.org/Research/Religion/wm413.cfm.

6. *Washington Times,* "Religion Under Secular Assault," April 13, 2005, by Julia Duin.

7. LifeSiteNews.com, "Homosexual Hate Crime Signed into Law: Chilling Effect on Free Speech, Religion and Importing Materials," Thursday, April 29, 2004, http://www.lifesite.net/ldn/2004/apr/04042901.html.

8. Stanley Kurtz, "Beyond Gay Marriage," *The Weekly Standard,* August 4, 2003.

9. Ibid.

10. Rod Parsley, *Silent No More,* (Charisma House, 2005), 144.

11. http:// www.2000gop.com/convention/speech/speechbush.html.

12. Amicus Brief, p. 1–2.

13. Chuck Colson, "Precedent Schmecedent," January 9, 2006, TownHall.org, http://townhall.com/opinion/column/chuckcolson/2006/01/09/ 181488.html.

14. Amicus Brief, p. 23.

15. Alan Sears and Craig Osten, *The ACLU vs. America: Exposing the Agenda to Redefine Moral Values,* (Nashville, Broadman & Holman Publishers, 2005).

16. Mark R. Levin, Men in Black: How the Supreme Court Is Destroying America, (Washington D.C.: Regnery, 2005).

CHAPTER 9

1. Robert I. Bradshaw, *Bending the Church to Save the World: The Welsh Revival of 1904* (1995, no copyright/public domain).

2. Rimas J. Orentas, *George Whitefield: Lightning Rod of the Great Awakening,* http://dylee.keel.econ.ship.edu/UBF/leaders/whitfild.htm.

3. Charles Finney, *What Is Revival?,* public domain.

4. Ronald J. Sider, *The Scandal of the Evangelical Conscience: Why Are Christians Living Just Like the Rest of the World?* (Grand Rapids, Michigan: Baker Books, 2005), 17.

5. John R. W. Stott, *Human Rights and Human Wrongs: Major Issues for a New Century* (Baker Books, 1999), 21.

6. Robert Lewis, *The Church of Irresistible Influence* (Grand Rapids, Michigan: Zondervan, 2001), 208.

7. Ibid., 210.

8. Evan Roberts, *Overcomer Magazine,* "The Successful Intercessor," September 1913.

9. R. A. Torrey, as cited in *Who Said That?,* compiled by George Sweeting (Chicago: Moody Press, 1994), 383.

10. Stephen Mansfield, *Forgotten Founding Father: The Heroic Legacy of George Whitefield* (Nashville: Cumberland House Publishing, 2001).

11. Noel Gibbard, *Fire on the Altar: A History and Evaluation of the 1904-05 Welsh Revival,* (Bryntirion Press, 2006).

CHAPTER 10

1. Silent No More, p. 65.
2. Francis Schaeffer, as cited in *Who Said That?*, George Sweeting (Chicago: Moody Press, 1985), 79.
3. George Barna, "Stewardship," http://www.barna.org/FlexPage.aspx?Page=Topic&TopicID=36.
4. John L. and Sylvia Ronsville, *The State of Church Giving Through 2001* (Empty Tomb, 2003), 12.
5. Ibid.
6. Robert Lewis, *The Church of Irresistible Influence* (Grand Rapids, Michigan: Zondervan, 2001), 79.
7. Charles Colson, *The Good Life: Seeking Purpose and Meaning and Truth in Your Life* (Wheaton, Illinois: Tyndale House, 2005), 133f.
8. President George W. Bush in a speech at the first White House National Conference on Faith-Based and Community Initiatives, June 1, 2004.
9. Pastor David Deters, Alger Park CRC, Grand Rapids, MI, http://www.kidshopeusa.org/Brix?pageID=431.
10. Robert Lewis with Rob Wilkins, *The Church of Irresistible Influence*, (Grand Rapids, MI: Zondervan, 2001).
11. Marvin Olasky, Herbert Schlossberg, Pierre Berthoud, Clark Pinnock, *Freedom, Justice and Hope: Toward a Strategy for the Poor and the Oppressed*, (Westchester, IL: Good News Publishers, 1988).
12. Marvin Olasky, *Renewing American Compassion: How Compassion for the Needy Can Turn Ordinary Citizens into Heroes*, (Washington D.C.: Regnery, 1997).

CHAPTER 11

1. Loren Cunningham, Youth With A Mission, "Spheres of Influence" (2003), http://www.ywamconnect.com/sites/Founders/LorenVintageMessages?multcontentitemid=6887.
2. James Garfield, "A Century of Congress," published in *Atlantic*, July 1877.
3. Nancy Benac, The Washington Post, "Justice Kennedy Holds Key to High Court", October 21, 2006, http://www.washingtonpost.com/wp-dyn/content/article/2006/10/21/AR2006102100371.html.

4. Bruce Fein, The Washington Times, "Genuine Turning Point", November 8, 2005, http://www.washingtontimes.com/commentary/20051107-100012-1331r.htm.

5. Columbus Citizen-Journal, March 25, 1985   George R. Plagenz, "Minister Makes It a Moving Service."

6. Charles Colson and Nancy Pearcey, *How Now Shall We Live?* (Wheaton, Illinois: Tyndale House, 1999), 466.

7. Roy Herron, *Can a Christian Influence Politics?: How to make a difference in Government,* (Tyndale House, 2005).

8. Randy Woodley, *Living in Color: Embracing God's Passion for Ethnic Diversity,* (Downers Grove, IL: Inter-varsity Press, 2004).

9. Clarence Shuler, *Winning the Race to Unity: Is Racial Reconciliation Really Working?* (Chicago, IL: Moody Publishers, 1998).

CHAPTER 12

1. Tom Brokaw, *The Greatest Generation* (Random House, 1998), 1.

2. Neil Postman, *Amusing Ourselves to Death: Public Discourse in the Age of Show Business* (Penguin Books, 1985).